F̲_____ of

FACES

F A C E S

Andrea Midgett

With photographs by Jean-Claude Lejeune

A DIVISION OF CTi
CampusLife
BOOKS
TYNDALE HOUSE
PUBLISHERS, INC.
WHEATON, ILLINOIS

"Alive Again" by Norman Habel is taken from *Interrobang* by Norman Habel, copyright 1969 by Fortress Press. Used by permission.

"The Wind" and "You" by Marilee Zdenek are taken from *God Is a Verb* by Marilee Zdenek and Marge Champion, copyright 1974 by Word Book Publishers. Used by permission.

All poetry by Ruth Senter is taken from a book by Ruth Senter to be published by Zondervan Publishing House in the spring of 1988.

All Bible quotations are taken from *The Holy Bible,* New International Version, copyright 1973, 1978 by the New York International Bible Society.

Cover photograph by Jack Hollingsworth

First printing, April 1987
Library of Congress Catalog Card Number 86-51484
ISBN 0-8423-0827-X, cloth
ISBN 0-8423-0826-1, paper
Copyright 1987 by Campus Life Books, a division of CTi
All rights reserved
Printed in the United States of America

Contents

FACES

SPRINGING

Father God,

I celebrate you and your world.

I clap my hands with the leaves of the trees

and sing with the birds in their branches.

Thank you for the gently warm bathing of the sun,

which is even now washing away the weariness

of this spinning day of world.

Thank you for the filling fullness of you,

terrible-tender in this world of empty men.

Thank you for your hand

in which we all are held,

in which the world turns

round and old and brown,

then new and green and you.

Creator of the woman me maybe me mostly me amazing me,

I celebrate you in me, making me me.

I shout *glory* with the silent rays of sun

and leap with the greenly spirits of the trees and grasses,

praising you whom I cannot begin to imagine,

you who imagined it all.

SANNA BAKER

He wraps himself in light as with a garment; he stretches out the heavens like a tent and lays the beams of his upper chambers on their waters. He makes the clouds his chariot and rides on the wings of the wind. He set the earth on its foundations; it can never be moved. You covered it with the deep as with a garment; the waters stood above the mountains. How many are your works, O Lord! In wisdom you made them all; the earth is full of your creatures. When you send your Spirit, they are created, and you renew the face of the earth.

PSALM 104:2, 3, 5, 6, 24, 30

When was the last time you exulted in being alive? It's easy to grow so weighed down with everyday concerns—school and friends and family—that you forget how remarkable life is. Just think about how complex you are, and how you've changed physically since you were born. Consider how quickly your moods can be affected by a song on the radio or a phone call from an interested friend. Ponder the worlds of insects or plants or animals or marine life, each unfathomable in detail and mystery.

An ungrateful spirit for life can be a sign of self-absorption. Ironically, those who make it a habit to offer thanks seem continually to find something to be thankful for. And, like Scrooge, those who are miserly in gratitude and wonderment become poorer and poorer in spirit.

Dear God, thank you for the wild diversity of life. Thank you for caring meticulously over each element, including me. Amen.

STEPPING OUT

It's like

jumping into an icy mountain stream

from dry, hot rocks;

rolling out of a warm sleeping bag

into a cold morning;

turning the shower off

and stepping out;

going off the high dive

for the first time;

not reaching for another potato chip;

typing the first word

of the term paper you are writing;

pushing yourself off a cliff

because there is no other way down.

Trusting God is hard to do.

RUTH SENTER

Find rest, O my soul, in God alone; my hope comes from him. He alone is my rock and my salvation; he is my fortress, I will not be shaken. My salvation and my honor depend on God; he is my mighty rock, my refuge. Trust in him at all times, O people; pour out your hearts to him, for God is our refuge.

PSALM 62:5-8

Surely God is my salvation; I will trust and not be afraid. The Lord, the Lord, is my strength and my song; he has become my salvation.

ISAIAH 12:2

It's difficult to trust anyone. Especially someone we hardly know. When two strangers meet, there is no trust between them. But as the two learn more about each other and share experiences, trust, like a bridge, is built between them.

God wants to be the bridge between you and him. But he doesn't expect your blind trust. He asks instead that you consider how he has proven himself. Through the ages, he loved and led and provided for mankind. In your life, he brought blessings and protection. He is there when you acknowledge him and he is there when you don't. You can trust God because of his record. What's more, as you share experiences you'll find that it's easier to trust him. And when you fail in your end of the trust bargain, he'll fill in the gap.

Dear God, help me to give my fears and hopes and dreams to you. Help me to trust fully in your love and plans for me. Amen.

BIG PICTURE

I.

From my window seat

my concerns shrink away

and I begin to see

my world in perspective.

I never feel as truly free

as when I am looking down on the earth

from the window seat of a jet.

The way it affects me is magical.

One moment I am the hurried pedestrian,

caught up in the hurricane whirl

of last-minute details.

Anxious. Distracted.

Then the transformation begins:

I step aboard the gleaming aircraft

and sink into my seat by the oblong window.

Engines complaining in a supersonic whine, we arrow

into the sky with a bump and a roar.

As the earth drops away, people,

houses, and cars shrink.

Cities dwindle and the land spreads out

laced with shimmering rivers

and the brown patchwork of farmland.

All the things that were so pressing

only minutes before now seem insignificant.

I am airborne. Free.

My concerns, like the world below,

have shrunk away;

they are mere specks on the distant horizon.

It is here that I begin to see

my life as God sees it:

Totally. In proper perspective.

He sees the road I am on,

where it has been,

where it is going.

He sees the rocky places ahead,

he knows the necessary detours

to bring me to my destination.

God is master of all ends and all beginnings.

Not just mine.

I am one of many travelers

whose footsteps he not only *sees,* but guides.

And though the roadways are all different,

the concern—his concern—is the same.

From my window-seat perspective I conclude

that my problems do not amount to very much—

And I am humbled that God loves me and cares for me.

STEVE LAWHEAD

The Lord delights in the way of the man whose steps he has made firm; though he stumble, he will not fall, for the Lord upholds him with his hand.

PSALM 37:23, 24

In his heart a man plans his course, but the Lord determines his steps.

PROVERBS 16:9

The Lord will fulfill his purpose for me.

PSALM 138:8

It's easy to grow so wrapped up in the complexities of our own lives that we lose perspective. Not that our problems aren't significant. Deciding on a career direction, for instance, is frightening. But such fears don't come close to those of a high-school cancer victim. Struggling to make the grades for an academic scholarship requires discipline and sweat. But the student fighting to overcome several generations of poverty must sweat more. When we take time to think of the many tremendous problems that others face, ours will lose their inflated importance.

It's not that we should be unconcerned or fatalistic about the future—we do play a role in what lies ahead. But we shouldn't be so consumed with making our own way that we deny God's role in shaping our lives. He knows how important the decisions and questions we face are. And he knows what ultimately lies ahead for each of us. With God's perspective, we'll be able to weigh our problems fairly and go forward with a sense of peace.

Dear God, help me to trust you more with my concerns for the future. And help me to remember those who face greater struggles than I. Amen.

BIG PICTURE

II.

God is working to bring the Big Picture

into final harmony with his plan,

but he is also working in me

to create an inner harmony.

Like a symphony conductor he directs a great orchestra,

blending innumerable individual notes

from a billion different

instruments into one grand melody.

He hears the orchestra and he hears each player

because he knows each part by heart.

Note by solitary note.

God is an artist creating a design

on an infinite canvas;

I am just one small part of that design.

The artist is working toward his purpose, not mine.

Yet simultaneously, what's good for the total design

is good for each individual element.

For me.

Consider a giant clock high in a tower.

Imagine the gears and cogs and wheels—

some as big as barn doors,

others small enough to hold in your fist.

We could say, "To be one small cog

on a larger gear within a

greater wheel means I do not have to be

the entire clock.

I am free to be what I am—part of the whole.

I am not responsible for how well the clock keeps time,

only how well I keep my place."

But this illustration shows

merely part of the Big Picture.

This is the paradox of God's love:

He makes each small part

the most important part;

he sees the complex interworkings of the Big Picture and

he sees each individual detail simultaneously, equally.

God's greater good—

the ultimate purpose of his grand design—

is my good, too.

When I realize that, I am truly free.

People dream of freedom.

And they picture it in different ways.

For me it is enough

from time to time to view the world

from the window seat of a jet streaking skyward.

To see people, cars, and houses shrink,

and cities dwindle,

and the land spread out broad and wide,

offering me a glimpse of God's Big Picture.

STEVE LAWHEAD

Just as each of us has one body with many members, and these members do not all have the same function, so in Christ we who are many form one body, and each member belongs to all the others.

ROMANS 12:4, 5

Come, let us sing for joy to the Lord; let us shout aloud to the Rock of our salvation. Let us come before him with thanksgiving and extol him with music and song. For the Lord is the great God, the great King above all gods. In his hand are the depths of the earth, and the mountain peaks belong to him. The sea is his, for he made it, and his hands formed the dry land. Come, let us bow down in worship, let us kneel before the Lord our Maker; for he is our God and we are the people of his pasture, the flock under his care.

PSALM 95:1-7

God orders the workings of the universe in all its vast and unexplained complexities—from ocean depths to the far reaches of space. Yet the Bible says that God also is aware of a single falling sparrow. Details don't pass him by. Though you sometimes may feel lost among the billions of people who inhabit our planet, you are known thoroughly by God. He has planned your way. He knows your needs and your future.

The complications of your personal life are not dwarfed in God's sight by those of the entire universe. He cares about the most minute problems you face: The teacher who harasses you for being "religious"; the friend who laughs behind your back. You, the individual, are as important to God as tens of thousands of people. And, unlike humans who can love only so many other humans so much, God has great love for you which doesn't lessen his love for others.

Dear God, thank you for your great love and knowledge and understanding of me. Thank you for caring about me in every way. Amen.

STILL LISTENING

If I sat here
in the middle of this room
letting the thoughts
come and go,
maybe the sounds of my soul
would reverberate off the walls
and the words
could be more clearly heard
in God's reply.
Wisdom, so often
I have shielded my heart
from the touching of your truth
in folly.
Still, I can hear your voice
amid
the creak
of the see and saw of my heart.
And above the music
kibitzing on
how I should
play the game,
your call pulls me toward
the road
where ultimate freedom lies.

MARIE HILLAN

Pay attention and listen to the sayings of the wise; apply your heart to what I teach, for it is pleasing when you keep them in your heart and have all of them ready on your lips. So that your trust may be in the Lord, I teach you today, even you.

PROVERBS 22:17-19

If any of you lacks wisdom, he should ask God, who gives generously to all without finding fault, and it will be given to him.

JAMES 1:5

You may never have heard God speak to you audibly, but that doesn't mean he is silent. His Spirit speaks to you, telling you when you've spoken too harshly or have been mean and self-serving. Your conscience, encouraging you to stop and talk with an elderly neighbor for a few minutes, can be thought of as God's messenger. The Scripture passage reminding you to be honest with your money is God's Word. Your Christian friends, discussing what their position should be on a controversial issue, give voice to the body of Christ.

Through the written and spoken word, God reminds us how we represent him on earth; he hasn't left us to our own musings. Wisdom—the ability to know how to live and think and feel—is of God. But we can tune him out. We can allow the world's discordant noises to overwhelm us. God still speaks today, if we're willing to listen.

Dear God, thank you for not being distant and silent. Forgive me for denying your voice, for crowding it out when I don't want to hear you. Amen.

YOU BE YOU

We watch the summer boats—

distant scraps of white and red and yellow on blue—

and you talk of what makes Melissa cry,

and I worry about all the universe.

The damp wind chills—

we slide down wet, black rocks

and hold each other.

A mist from the spray

reaches out at our faces,

but can't squeeze between them—

pressed together.

We're pressed together, close,

but you are you,

and I'm beginning to be me.

I watch a little boy,

who runs like a frightened kitten,

launching his kite.

No good; its nose bumps rocks.

The boy stands drooped

like a nude dandelion stem,

and I see a symbol of all of us,

of me.

And you?

You see a little boy to help,

and tug me toward him.

We had lunch one day

with a girl I'd known for months.

You'd never met her before,

but later you told me

why she just picked at her sandwich,

and why she talked about herself.

I'd been oblivious,

living in my abstractions,

while you see to the core of people.

Be free

to be.

To be yourself, Lover.

Imitating me

would be a waste of you.

God made you

a master painting for me to study

—not a mirror.

HAROLD MYRA

For you created my inmost being; you knit me together in my mother's womb.

PSALM 139:13

But the Lord said to Samuel, "Do not consider his appearance or his height, for I have rejected him. The Lord does not look at the things man looks at. Man looks at the outward appearance, but the Lord looks at the heart."

1 SAMUEL 16:7

Working to understand yourself will make understanding other people easier. If you learn to identify your own insecurities, you'll recognize the insecurities of others. When you can admit to your own fears, you'll better understand the fears of someone else. On the other hand, if you don't work at self-understanding, you'll have little success understanding other people. The simple solution will be to make quick, harsh judgments and to expect everyone to please you.

God sees right into every individual's heart. Vision like his should be your goal. But it has to start with the hardest person of all—you. When you've learned to be honest about who you are, you'll better know and accept others for who they are.

Dear God, thank you for understanding my problems and doubts and fears—and my strengths and joys, as well. Help me to see others with your eyes. Amen.

HANGING BY A C

Sometimes I feel like an information machine.

Plug me in and watch me go.

You can program me for anything:

 "Memorize this list,

  these names,

  those dates . . .

 and chapters one through five.

 There will be a test on Monday."

Test. I hate that word.

It means pressure and fear.

What if I don't measure up?

What if I fail?

My whole life hangs by a C.

So I study,

and read

and study some more.

The hours crawl away,

and the pages stare back.

My eyes go fuzzy and attention drifts. . . .

 Ten million years of life on this planet

 and I'm memorizing geometry theorems!

 What's it all for?

No matter how well I do,

Somebody else does better,

knows more, scores higher.

The "achievers" get the good grades;

I'm no match for them. Why even compete?

Competition—that's my problem. Not failure.

I want to be the *best*. The brightest.

I want everyone to look up to me and marvel at my intellect.

That's wrong, I know it. Deep down I know it.

Test scores and grading curves

have nothing to do with the kind of person I am.

If I were the only kid taking the test

in a room by myself, a class of one,

how much recognition could I gain?

None.

There would be no winners, no losers, no game.

The next test, I'll be the "only one" taking it.

I want it to be a challenge

not a contest.

STEVE LAWHEAD

Yet when I surveyed all that my hands had done and what I had toiled to achieve, everything was meaningless, a chasing after the wind; nothing was gained under the sun. . . . For without him, who can eat or find enjoyment?

Age should speak; advanced years should teach wisdom. But it is the spirit in a man, the breath of the Almighty, that gives him understanding. It is not only the old who are wise, not only the aged who understand what is right.

JOB 32:7-9

At times, other people's expectations—parents', teachers', friends', even God's—make us uncomfortable. But we also put tremendous pressure on ourselves. We push to conform to our personal image of a successful, happy, together person. We must be the best academically, socially, physically, spiritually. We must make every team, charm every member of the opposite sex, please every adult, ace every exam—or we've failed.

It is important to push ahead as individuals; we should always be expanding and growing and learning. But to subject ourselves to relentless personal pressure can easily backfire. To lose all sense of self-worth because we flunked an algebra test or because we didn't make the cheerleading squad is to rate ourselves only in terms of our abilities. And that is to deny the value God places on us as his creations, unique human beings. God's love for us remains constant—whether we can balance an equation or not.

Dear God, thank you for valuing me regardless of my successes and failures in life. Help me to have realistic expectations for myself. Amen.

29

EMANCIPATION

The gateway to living

flung open

by a cross

and

a hand

horribly

scarred

beckons please come

to Me.

JOY NELSON

I tell you the truth, the man who does not enter the sheep pen by the gate, but climbs in by some other way, is a thief and a robber. I am the gate; whoever enters through me will be saved. He will come in and go out, and find pasture. The thief comes only to steal and kill and destroy; I have come that they may have life, and have it to the full.
JOHN 10:1, 9, 10

See, I have engraved you on the palms of my hands.
ISAIAH 49:16

In the rush of school and part-time jobs and ball clubs and church and friends and parents and band practice and everything else in life, it's easy to overlook the simplicity of the gospel. Christ died for our sins. My sins. Your sins. His hands, scarred with the reality of death, are open to all who will come to him. He offers life to every person, life abundant and free.

But we make Christ complex. We devise elaborate methods to make our way to him, ignoring his outstretched hands ever before us. We crowd him out of our lives with ceaseless activity and say that *he* is unapproachable. We build walls around ourselves, and blame our prisonlike existence on Christianity. God has provided the answer for all mankind. It is we who complicate matters.

Dear God, forgive me for tripping over the simple message of Christ. And thank you for catching me when I fall. Amen.

THE RIDDLE

I feel it every now and then,

The rhymed vibration of a voice

Seeping in through the stuttered cracks

Of my sin-hardened soul.

Why it comes and where it comes from

I need only guess to know.

But it seems to be a secret signal

Sent far

And long ago,

A coded message come to earth

From beyond the pilot-star,

Tapped out in the form of a simple riddle . . .

Tell me that you love me—

I'll tell you who you are.

STEVE LAWHEAD

But ask the animals, and they will teach you, or the birds of the air, and they will tell you; or speak to the earth, and it will teach you, or let the fish of the sea inform you. Which of all these does not know that the hand of the Lord has done this? In his hand is the life of every creature and the breath of all mankind.

JOB 12:7-10

Yet he has not left himself without testimony: He has shown kindness by giving you rain from heaven and crops in their seasons; he provides you with plenty of food and fills your hearts with joy.

ACTS 14:17

Every person considers God at some point in his or her life. Even if one has never heard of Jesus Christ, nature suggests the possibility of a creator; God left his signature in the world. And he left a void within each of us that only he can fill.

When talking with friends about your faith, ask them what they think about God. Give them a chance to express their questions and doubts. They may believe that God set the world in motion, but that he is not interested or involved with everyday existence. Or, they may believe in God but not in Jesus Christ. Your friends' thoughts often demonstrate God's interest in them; he is constantly trying to reach through to individuals. The voice in a person's heart suggesting that God exists and that he wants to be in relationship with him or her is that of God's Spirit. God desires that all people come to know him through his Son.

Help others recognize his voice.

Dear God, thank you for making yourself known to me, for I could never find you on my own. May I be instrumental in others meeting you. Amen.

A MAN WENT FREE

A man went free the day you died.

Barabbas.

Hero. Macho Man.

The People's Choice.

They cut his chains and

    buried his past in his empty prison cell.

Murder. Insurrection.

It didn't matter.

But they nailed you down,

Strapped you with the weight of a cross

While he walked away clean.

They restored his dignity to him.

Free man. Pardoned. No more labels.

But they stripped you,

Gave you thorns for your crown,

A weed for your scepter

And a line in the obituary column that read:

JESUS. KING OF THE JEWS.

They shouted his name through the city:

Blazed it in neon lights

    and put a marquee around it

While they drove you to the place of the Skull,

Gave you vinegar to drink

and threw dice for your clothing.

When darkness came,

You bowed your head and died alone

While he celebrated in the streets

   with the Passover crowd.

A man went free the day you died.

I was that man.

RUTH SENTER

He was pierced for our transgressions, he was crushed for our iniquities; the punishment that brought us peace was upon him, and by his wounds we are healed. We all, like sheep, have gone astray, each of us has turned to his own way; and the Lord has laid on him the iniquity of us all.

ISAIAH 53:5, 6

He himself bore our sins in his body on the tree, so that we might die to sins and live for righteousness; by his wounds you have been healed.

1 PETER 2:24

Barabbas seems an extreme representative. After all, we aren't criminals. In fact, when compared to most other people we come off pretty clean. But there's a problem: God's point of reference is himself. To compare his holiness and our pretensions of being good is like placing the sun against a ten-cent sparkler. Cheating, lying to parents, gossiping, using people—it's all against God's character. In every way we're more like Barabbas, a fellow human being, than we are like God. Given the same circumstances, we could easily be in Barabbas's place. (Maybe he had a lousy home life, maybe his friends exerted a bad influence, maybe he was working to change society in the only way he saw available.)

The sin Christ died for was Barabbas's sin and every man's sin—past, present, and future. It was the weight of every man's sin that drove the nails into Christ's palms and feet.

Dear God, forgive me for my sins against you and against my neighbor. Forgive me for the part I played in your Son's death. Amen.

WHAT IS GOD REALLY LIKE?

I.

G–O–D

Three simple letters
strung together
to form a familiar word
I've tossed around since childhood:

GOD.

I've probably known the word
longer than, say,
corn flakes
or tuberculosis.
But what is God really like?
Is he old or young?
I rather think of him as old;
he's been around awhile.
But the idea of divinity aging
doesn't quite fit.
God should be virile,
energetic,
jogging through space in sweats
to get things done,

not sitting on a bentwood rocker

in robe and slippers

three gasps away

from cardiac arrest.

GOD.

Is he fun-loving

or prudish?

As startlingly diverse and creative

as his world is,

he hardly seems the type

to squelch parties.

But to think of him chortling

with the guys over a coarse joke

is unimaginable.

So, I assume,

his idea of fun *must* at times

run crosswise with mine.

And yet, that he sits around all day being good

makes me wonder: *Does God get bored?*

What does he do with his time?

He seems to have a lot of it

on his hands.

Yet it seems unlikely

he would procrastinate

and dawdle through

his cosmic tasks

just to stretch them out

over another millennium or two.

But what is time to God?

When I think of him,

really ponder him,

I sense my own limitations

more acutely

than ever.

JIM LONG

"For my thoughts are not your thoughts, neither are your ways my ways," declares the Lord. *"As the heavens are higher than the earth, so are my ways higher than your ways and my thoughts than your thoughts."*

ISAIAH 55:8, 9

Jesus cried out, "When a man believes in me, he does not believe in me only, but in the one who sent me. When he looks at me, he sees the one who sent me."

JOHN 12:44, 45

GOD. Three everyday letters whose sound is quickly flipped off the tongue and consumed in space. Shouldn't God's name be grand-sounding and many-syllabled, at least as long as the names given to royalty? Or is it that God is more than the sum of our vocabularies; many words strung together cannot adequately grasp him?

GOD. The simplicity of the name resists a fluffed-up image. God is the King of kings, yes. And he is the worn carpenter. The most righteous judge. And the man wrongly accused.

GOD. We begin to know him through Bible study and prayer. We see him alive in the church and in Christians who flesh out his presence. We observe something of his character in the natural world. Most importantly, we meet God through his Son, Jesus Christ.

Names are meaningless in and of themselves. They gain significance as we understand who or what they represent. Make it your goal to know God. And to understand his name.

Dear God, may I call upon you by name as a friend well-known. Amen.

WHAT IS GOD REALLY LIKE?

II.

In my mind I need a picture of God,

a mural as broad as the sky.

Broader.

Instead, I carry around in my head

a crumpled snapshot—

the kind of photo

my grandpa used to take

with an old box camera:

blurry, dark, poorly composed.

"God is the one on the left.

I know you can't quite see him

(he's behind Uncle Harry),

but he is there."

God.

I see his fingerprints,

all over creation:

in swirling galaxies

and newborn aardvarks,

in craggy canyons

and kumquat trees.

I dig into his book,

leaf through tissue-thin pages

looking for ideas.

In his book I see more than

fingerprints,

I see a signature—his signature.

And in the curves of the letters

a story line emerges,

a plot unfolds.

I see what he's up to,

what he's like.

Not everyone buys the image

of God as writer,

renowned author.

But it seems only sensible,

so like God, to want to leave clear clues

for me to follow.

God.

Squinting through this Book of his,

I see something

that shouldn't surprise me

at all,

but does;

I find something so logical,

so predictable,

that it takes me off guard in startled shock,

confirming as true

something that has been inevitable all along:

God is good.

Perfect.

And his expectations of me

arch high above my ability to deliver.

God is good.

I am not.

And he doesn't appreciate

the disparity.

JIM LONG

As the rain and the snow come down from heaven, and do not return to it without watering the earth and making it bud and flourish, so that it yields seed for the sower and bread for the eater, so is my word that goes out from my mouth: It will not return to me empty, but will accomplish what I desire and achieve the purpose for which I sent it.

ISAIAH 55:10, 11

In the beginning was the Word, and the Word was with God, and the Word was God. He was with God in the beginning. Through him all things were made; without him nothing was made that has been made. In him was life, and that life was the light of men. The light shines in the darkness, but the darkness has not understood it.

JOHN 1:1-5

The Bible is more than thousands of words on thousands of pages, written in thousands of languages for thousands of people. God is his Word. That's why the Bible is so powerful—it pulsates with God himself. It is not dead print. The Word of God is life-giving, or it is unlike God the Creator and sustainer of life. It is illuminating and directive, or it is unlike God the all-wise and all-knowing. The Word of God is authoritative, or it is unlike God the all-powerful and most-high Judge.

We can (and should) study the Bible. We can question it, take it apart, talk about its writers and their backgrounds and historical situations, but ultimately we accept or reject the Bible as God himself speaking to us. Since God says he is the living Word, what you think of one will necessarily affect what you think of the other.

Dear God, thank you for giving man your Word. As I search it, help me to better understand you, myself, and others. Let it teach me your way. Amen.

WHAT IS GOD REALLY LIKE?

III.

I hardly expected my search
for an inspiringly clear picture of God
to lead me back
to a discouragingly clear picture
of myself. Always, I have been aware of
my shortcomings.
No one has had to coax me
into acknowledging my
moral glitches.
What seems obvious to me now
has always seemed obvious:
The more I strive to be good,
the more elusive goodness seems.

"Be holy," the stellar writer says,
"because I am holy." He might just as well say:
"I am something that you
will never be,
can never be;
now, get on with the task
of being it!"
Or, he could have said:

"Walk on water!

But shoes with floats don't count."

The mystery is,

if God's book is to be believed,

he is always fiddling

with impossibilities,

twisting the unlikely

into the probable.

The Bible relates wild tales of God

teaching paralytics to sprint

and enabling blind folks to gawk

at the multicolored world.

How does God do it?

Mirrors?

Sleight of hand?

The stories reek of authenticity,

credibility.

I wonder:

Does God perform

moral tricks, too?

Can he pull perfection out of my life

as an illusionist dips

into a top hat

and yanks out a bunny by the ears?

God.

As I read between the lines

the moral mystery seems to unravel.

If God's lips seem to curl

into a faint smile as he urges me

on toward the impossible,

it may be because he plans to offer

his moral strength

at the very moment he shows me

my moral weakness.

He will help me improve;

he will also make up

the vast difference

between what I am

and what he expects me to be.

God will cover my blunders

with his free-flowing forgiveness.

But if I didn't first see my weaknesses,

I might never accept his strength.

So he doesn't let me off

the moral hook,

but he doesn't skewer me

with it either.

In the face of such

undeserved kindness,

I see the most complete picture

of this flawless friend.

And even a sky-sized mural

cannot contain it.

JIM LONG

The word of God is living and active. Sharper than any double-edged sword, it penetrates even to dividing soul and spirit, joints and marrow; it judges the thoughts and attitudes of the heart. Nothing in all creation is hidden from God's sight. Everything is uncovered and laid bare before the eyes of him to whom we must give account. Therefore, since we have a great high priest who has gone through the heavens, Jesus the Son of God, let us hold firmly to the faith we profess. For we do not have a high priest who is unable to sympathize with our weaknesses, but we have one who has been tempted in every way, just as we are—yet was without sin. Let us then approach the throne of grace with confidence, so that we may receive mercy and find grace to help us in our time of need.

HEBREWS 4:12-16

Our consciences tell us we need to improve. Parents and friends tell us we need to improve. And when we take a few minutes to be alone with God, he often tells us we need to improve. So much for the warm feelings of devotions. Why read the Bible and pray, if doing so only confirms (in a big way) our worst suspicions about ourselves? Why be more miserable than we already are? We know we can't live up to God's expectations, not 100 percent.

Nothing is ever improved upon until the truth is established. Athletes watch videos of themselves in action so they'll know what they did wrong and where they need to improve. Anorexics must recognize their physical and psychological condition before breaking self-destructive eating habits.

Likewise, our jealousies and insecurities and lusts won't be replaced with generosity and confidence and purity until we see ourselves as we really are and admit our need for change. That's why we go to the Bible: to meet God, and to meet ourselves. God uses his Word not as a hacksaw, but as a surgical tool. With it he exposes what he alone can remedy.

Dear God, through Bible study and prayer help me to see myself as you see me. And grant me your strength, that I may become a person who pleases you in every way. Amen.

IF LOVE WERE JUST A FEELING

Like a hot shot on a new-car shopping spree,

I'd check out your equipment,

if love were just a feeling.

I'd study all the external things—

the shape of your body, the style of your talk,

your humor and poise.

I'd judge by what I see, hear, touch,

if love were just a feeling.

Like two mannequins sharing a display case in silence,

I'd never really know you.

I'd ignore your humanness, deny your faults.

I'd exploit you, taking what you have,

what I want,

if love were just a feeling.

Like Swedish ivy intertwined,

I'd cling to you possessively.

And smothering you, I'd make our already superficial

relationship more shallow still,

if love were just a feeling.

Like a sportsman shooting white-water rapids,

I'd conquer you and move on,

if love were just a feeling.

Our relationship would surge,

invigorating but temporary.

There would be no commitment to hold me

when the inevitable conflicts would come,

if, for me, love were just a feeling.

JIM LONG

If I speak in the tongues of men and of angels, but have not
love, I am only a resounding gong or a clanging cymbal. If I
have the gift of prophecy and can fathom all mysteries and all
knowledge, and if I have a faith that can move mountains, but
have not love, I am nothing. If I give all I possess to the poor
and surrender my body to the flames, but have not love, I gain
nothing.

Love is patient, love is kind. It does not envy, it does not
boast, it is not proud. It is not rude, it is not self-seeking, it is
not easily angered, it keeps no record of wrongs. Love does
not delight in evil but rejoices with the truth. It always
protects, always trusts, always hopes, always perseveres.

Love never fails. But where there are prophecies, they will
cease; where there are tongues, they will be stilled; where
there is knowledge, it will pass away. For we know in part and
we prophesy in part, but when perfection comes, the
imperfect disappears. When I was a child, I talked like a child, I
thought like a child, I reasoned like a child. When I became a
man, I put childish ways behind me. Now we see but a poor
reflection; then we shall see face to face. Now I know in part;
then I shall know fully, even as I am fully known.

And now these three remain: faith, hope and love. But the
greatest of these is love.

1 CORINTHIANS 13

It's not inaccurate to think of love as a feeling. It's just incomplete. Sometimes you have feelings of love toward your family, sometimes you don't. Regardless, you know that you love them. "But that's families," you say. "When two people of the opposite sex love each other, feelings will be there." And that's true enough; the attraction between a man and a woman usually rides on strong emotions we call love.

But passion is not the essence of love, because feelings will come and go. Love is caring about another person in every way. It's wanting the best for another and respecting his or her individuality. It's a willingness to forsake our personal desires for those of the other person, desires we may not understand. In brief, love is commitment. And commitment costs. Consider Christ's love for us and what it cost him. His love didn't depend on feelings; it depended on his will to love us even when the love wasn't returned. Christ's model of love is one we should aspire to in all our relationships—his is complete love.

Dear God, thank you for the great example of love, Jesus Christ. Make his love for me the basis of my love for others, male or female. Amen.

THE TREE

Dark

as

death

Heavy

Thick

Splinter-

Grained

Wood

For God so loved the world

that he gave his one and only Son

That whoever believes in him

shall not perish

but have eternal life

Life

from

Dead

Wood

Fruit-

laden

Branches

and

Vines

Bright

and

Light

The

Cross

of

Christ.

G. M. WAKATAKE

I am the true vine and my Father is the gardener. He cuts off every branch in me that bears no fruit, while every branch that does bear fruit he trims clean so that it will be even more fruitful. I am the vine; you are the branches. If a man remains in me and I in him, he will bear much fruit; apart from me you can do nothing. If anyone does not remain in me, he is like a branch that is thrown away and withers; such branches are picked up, thrown into the fire and burned. If you remain in me and my words remain in you, ask whatever you wish, and it will be given you. This is to my Father's glory, that you bear much fruit, showing yourselves to be my disciples.

JOHN 15:1, 2, 5-8

If you're as fruitless as a dead tree branch, it may be that you're resisting God's work in your life. He knows how to prune you in such a way that you blossom for him. He calls himself the Gardener; he is the provider of light and air and water. To resist him is to be resigned to whatever life you can manufacture on your own. Are you growing up green for God?

Dear God, be the lifeblood that flows through me. Shape me into a tree grown tall and beautiful for you. Amen.

WHAT ABOUT QUESTIONS LIKE MINE?
BY PHILIP YANCEY

Sometimes I have the quick sensation

that my life is leaking away.

I want to experiment, to try things

my faith has always denied me.

I feel cramped and uptight.

I wonder what I'm missing

out on in life. There's a streak

inside me, a big one, that tells me

to find things out for myself,

not to rely on the Bible or

on other Christians for guidance.

**Whoever finds his life will lose it, and
whoever loses his life for my sake will find it.**
MATTHEW 10:39

Having just received my year-end

earnings stub, I looked back over a year's spending.

I pride myself in being generous

by helping the poor and giving to missions,

but I can find a lot of figures in my check

book that relate mainly to my

pleasure. I'm always saving for

"the future," just in case something

happens. Why do I struggle to cover

all the areas that might go wrong

financially? Why do I think

more about the price of gasoline

than about an earthquake in China?

So do not worry, saying, "What shall
we eat?" or "What shall we drink?"
or "What shall we wear?" For the pagans
run after all these things, and your
heavenly Father knows that you need them.
But seek first his kingdom and his righteousness,
and all these things will be given to you as well.
Therefore do not worry about tomorrow,
for tomorrow will worry about itself.
Each day has enough trouble of its own.

MATTHEW 6:31-34

Not long ago I met a four-year-old

dying of leukemia. I told the family

I'd pray, but now that the time's

come, I don't even know how to begin.

Should I pray for healing, as I

watch that tiny body deteriorate?

Should I pray for more faith?

For strength for the parents?

What can I say? So much of life

seems too complex for

intelligent prayer.

*In the same way, the Spirit helps us
in our weakness. We do not know what
we ought to pray, but the Spirit
himself intercedes for us with groans
that words cannot express. And he
who searches our hearts knows
the mind of the Spirit, because
the Spirit intercedes for the saints
in accordance with God's will.*

ROMANS 8:26, 27

I listened to a five-minute recap

of the news of the year. Earthquakes.

Wars. Hurricanes.

Crime and terrorism everywhere.

The world seems out of control.

No one seems interested

in working together.

*In this world you will have trouble.
But take heart! I have overcome the world.*

JOHN 16:33

It's been 2,000 years since anyone's

seen you in the flesh, Lord.

To some, each year makes your promises

seem a little more remote.

Our world of machines and sports

and fun seems so different

from the one you lived in. We

Christians who carry your name around

can feel pretty isolated from you.

What must it have been like to

be one of your followers and listen

to you standing in front of us,

undeniably real?

I will not leave you as orphans;
I will come to you. Before long,
the world will not see me anymore,
but you will see me. Because I live,
you also will live. On that day
you will realize that I am in my Father,
and you are in me, and I am in you.

JOHN 14:18-20

One last question, Lord.

Is it OK to have doubts like these?

We know that the whole creation
has been groaning as in the pains
of childbirth right up to the present time.
Not only so, but we ourselves,
who have the firstfruits of the Spirit,
groan inwardly as we wait eagerly
for our adoption as sons, the redemption
of our bodies. For in this hope we were saved.
But hope that is seen is no hope at all.
Who hopes for what he already has?
But if we hope for what we do not yet
have, we wait for it patiently.

ROMANS 8:22-25

Figuring out what it means to live, to reason, to act as a Christian in today's world is not easy. But perhaps it's never been easy, not for any group of people. And perhaps we're wrong to think that it should be. Struggling with complex and painful issues is a sign that the Spirit of God lives within you; he is working to make you more Christlike. Agonizing about the poor can spur you to help needy people in your city. Empathizing with the pains and fears of cancer victims can lead you to be a true friend to someone facing death. Take your questions to God, and ask him to help you find answers you can live with.

Dear God, create in me a heart that can feel the world's weightiness as you do. And help me find your answers to life's disturbing questions. Amen.

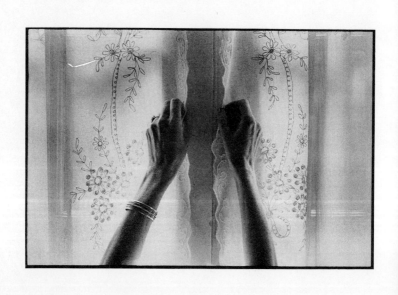

WAKE UP TO YOURSELF

I.

Just once—

tomorrow morning, maybe—

when you wake up,

your mouth tasting like wool

and the day outside your window

gray and unformed,

think about this.

Before you start remembering work you didn't get done,

or worrying whether to wear

that blue-striped thing or

the yellow one, or

wishing you had all the good looks

you'll never have; before all that,

think

Aren't there good reasons to be glad I'm

waking up as me?

Maybe you have

pimples

or feel short

or your nose is too big.

Ignore the little flaws;

see the big picture—

knit your hands together

and squeeze the fingers tight,

watch them glow red and

snap back to normal color when you let go.

Stretch your toes to the foot of the bed—

your body works.

It works like a marvel, a dream—

faster than thought it does what

you want.

No levers, no steering wheel;

you think and it's there.

A ball sails high in the air and

in a second your brain solves

a half-hour's calculus problem.

You think, "I've got it!"

and your body is already

on its way to gather it in.

Without calculation

a huge muscle called your heart

accelerates

to bathe every cell

(billions of them) with blood

and your lungs scoop the air

for oxygen

and harvest your blood

for carbon dioxide.

It doesn't happen just

catching a ball.

It happens walking down the hall

or springing from bed in the morning,

joyful to be

in your own body.

TIM STAFFORD

Then God said, "Let us make man in our image, in our likeness, and let them rule over the fish of the sea and the birds of the air, over the livestock, over all the earth, and over all the creatures that move along the ground." So God created man in his own image, in the image of God he created him; male and female he created them.

GENESIS 1:26, 27

I praise you because I am fearfully and wonderfully made; your works are wonderful, I know that full well.

PSALM 139:14

Some attitudes haven't changed much. Society continues to rank people based on their looks, as though a person has something to do with the shape of his mouth or the size of her ears, length of legs or color of eyes. Nice looks are just that—nice to look at, nothing more and nothing less. We should know better than to assign beauty unwarranted value. Think of the many well-known beautiful people whose lives are totally self-centered, who have been exploited by others, or who have wrongly relied on looks to get them by in life. Or consider your own looks; you know the real you is beneath your skin and bones.

Whether we are tall, short, heavy, or skinny, our value and self-worth lie in the fact that we were created by God, in his image. Instead of basing our opinion of ourselves and others on the basis of looks (or even brains), we should base it on the wonder of who we are. We can run and cry and taste ice cream and program computers and write music. We are marvelous because the Creator made us so.

Dear God, thank you for the value I have as part of your creation. Help me to recognize the value you give to others. Amen.

WAKE UP TO YOURSELF

II.

Take a minute now:

count to yourself

all the people you'll talk to today—

teachers, friends, parents,

brothers, sisters.

Have you ever gone twenty-four hours

without talking to someone?

Each person on earth (billions of them)

is as much a marvel as you;

yet each person needs others.

We work together:

I don't have to reinvent arithmetic

to count my socks,

or plant wheat seeds

in order to eat bread next September.

Someone else has already done those things.

Is there a radio near your bed?

Turn it on and another amazing creature will

tell you the weather.

He got it from another

wonderful creature

who got it from instruments

made by another

and invented by yet another wonderful creature

who isn't even alive anymore.

How well off would you be

if this cold morning

you had to do everything alone:

make your own food,

house,

socks,

car?

Where would you be without all those unseen people?

Isn't it incredible

how we share?

One minute more

before you get out of bed.

Think about one more thing.

Giraffes move gracefully;

bees share the invention of honey;

an antelope leaps quicker than you can think.

But no other animal

so far as I know

ever lies awake

in the gray morning,

eyes wide open,

amazed, thinking

how wonderful it is to wake up

as me.

TIM STAFFORD

From heaven the Lord looks down and sees all mankind; from his dwelling place he watches all who live on earth—he who forms the hearts of all, who considers everything they do.

PSALM 33:13-15

O Lord, you have searched me and you know me. You know when I sit and when I rise; you perceive my thoughts from afar. You discern my going out and my lying down; you are familiar with all my ways. Before a word is on my tongue you know it completely, O Lord. How precious to me are your thoughts, O God! How vast is the sum of them! Were I to count them, they would outnumber the grains of sand. When I awake, I am still with you.

PSALM 139:1-4, 17, 18

As you grow to become independent, it would be easy to forget how connected you are with other people. But even gaining independence requires the help of others. Your parents taught you the rudiments of health and personal care when you were a child. Other adults are teaching you, formally or by example, how to fulfill specific job assignments. The car you drive, the frozen meals you warm, the tennis shoes you lace every morning—they all help you toward independence; they all are the work of others.

It's a paradox: You're connected with those who lived before you, who live now, and who will live in the future; yet you are your own person. No one else in the world is exactly like you. So instead of pushing yourself to be a mirror of your friends, and instead of criticizing others when they don't conform to your image of who they should be, thank God for the connected-yet-separateness of mankind. God delights in the diversity and continuity of his creation. We should do the same.

71

Dear God, thank you for all the people who contribute to my life, many whom I don't even know. Thank you for what we share as people, and for what makes us distinct from one another. Amen.

IF I REALLY CARED . . .

I'd look you in the eyes when you talk to me;

I'd think about what you're saying rather than what I'm going

to say next;

I'd hear your feelings as well as your words.

If I really cared . . .

I'd listen without defending;

I'd hear without deciding whether you're right or wrong;

I'd ask you why, not just how and when and where.

If I really cared . . .

I'd allow you inside of me;

I'd tell you my hopes, my dreams, my fears, my hurts;

I'd tell you where I've blown it and when I've made it.

If I really cared . . .

I'd laugh with you but not at you;

I'd talk with you and not to you;

And I'd know when it's time to do neither.

If I really cared . . .

I wouldn't climb over your walls;

I'd hang around until you let me in the gate.

I wouldn't unlock your secrets;

I'd wait until you handed me the key.

If I really cared . . .

    I'd love you anyhow;

    But I'd ask for the best that you can give

    And gently draw it from you.

If I really cared . . .

    I'd put my scripts away,

    And leave my solutions at home.

    The performances would end.

    We'd be ourselves.

RUTH SENTER

Yet I am writing you a new command; its truth is seen in him and you, because the darkness is passing and the true light is already shining. Anyone who claims to be in the light but hates his brother is still in the darkness. Whoever loves his brother lives in the light, and there is nothing in him to make him stumble. But whoever hates his brother is in the darkness and walks around in the darkness; he does not know where he is going, because the darkness has blinded him.

1 JOHN 2:8-11

There is a friend who sticks closer than a brother.

PROVERBS 18:24

Rejoice with those who rejoice; mourn with those who mourn.

ROMANS 12:15

Friendship is based on the staying power of love. It isn't just being around for the good times. Real friendship is being there during the bad and the medium, ho-hum times as well—the times when love requires effort and discipline. To listen (perhaps again and again), to respond appropriately, to share the weight of a friend's anguish is demanding. You have to forget your own needs and put those of your friend first.

During his earthly life, Christ offered friendship. He celebrated with his friends in times of joy, and he cried with them when confronted with grief. Christ knew how to be a friend for the ups and downs of everyday life. Today we are the living extensions of his friendship. For us, to walk with him is to walk with others.

Dear God, thank you for the friendship you offer me through your Son. May the friendship I extend to others be of the same quality. Amen.

LIBERATE ME

Liberate me, Lord, from this self-made prison

That binds me close like

Bars of steel.

The key is Jesus,

And the turning in the lock is "I believe."

MARY A. JOHNSON

To the Jews who had believed him, Jesus said, "If you hold to my teaching, you are really my disciples. Then you will know the truth, and the truth will set you free." They answered him, "We are Abraham's descendants and have never been slaves of anyone. How can you say that we shall be set free?" Jesus replied, "I tell you the truth, everyone who sins is a slave to sin. Now a slave has no permanent place in the family, but a son belongs to it forever. So if the Son sets you free, you will be free indeed."

JOHN 8:31-36

The most difficult person we live with every day is ourself. For we continually frustrate the attempts of the Holy Spirit to liberate us from our sin. We form habits that drag us down like chains on an eagle's leg—then we think we can't fly. We doubt our capabilities until we're convinced we can't get off the ground. We allow society to keep our dreams and aspirations earthbound. In short, we live in self-made cages.

Christ said that only in his truth will we find liberty. He came to set us free, to release us from our sin, to release what humanity continues to bind. However, freedom is taxing as well as exhilarating. Christ takes the chains away, but we have to want the heights badly enough to try our wings. The alternative is to remain grounded for life.

Dear God, thank you for paying the price to set me free. May I readily accept the responsibilities of freedom. Amen.

REVERSAL

God, I give up.

You win this match.

Someone said

following love

may mean the destruction of

your dreams.

But it's also the fulfillment

of a more magnificent dream

you haven't had yet.

Next time I challenge you,

wrestle me 'til I drop—

spent,

breathless,

dead.

Then resurrect me

in your dream.

MICHAEL SARES

My son, do not despise the Lord's discipline and do not resent his rebuke, because the Lord disciplines those he loves, as a father the son he delights in.

PROVERBS 3:11, 12

Our fathers disciplined us for a little while as they thought best; but God disciplines us for our good, that we may share in his holiness. No discipline seems pleasant at the time, but painful. Later on, however, it produces a harvest of righteousness and peace for those who have been trained by it.

HEBREWS 12:10, 11

Love is demanding; it wants the best for the beloved. If you raise a puppy, you'll teach it to come when called. To let it run wild would be too risky: a puppy is no match for a car. But you can't tell the puppy that, you can only work to make it obedient, confident that you're loving it even if the puppy isn't quite so sure. You'll review the same lessons again and again. Loving a puppy enough to teach it to obey will require your commitment, time, and patience.

Likewise, God's love—so immense that we cannot comprehend its implications—is demanding. It cost him and it costs us. God's goal is to make us more like himself; with love he is continually shaping us. God's love chases us down before we destroy our lives with personal fears, inhibitions, and anxieties. His love tears away our inflated self-images so we can know the value he gives us. Because God knows what lies ahead, he trains and disciplines us to recognize and obey him, though we may not understand why. To be loved by God is to bear the mark of his discipline and training.

Dear God, thank you for loving me enough to teach me your ways. May I be a willing student, one who trusts in your wisdom and foresight. Amen.

RESCUE

Lord,

When do I come to you for help?

The moment I hear the five-day advanced forecast?

When I hear the ten o'clock report the evening before?

When I feel the first uncomfortable breeze,

or see the first dark cloud on the horizon?

Or do I wait until the sky turns into clouds?

Until the raindrops rattle the window pane?

Until my furniture begins to float?

Lord, you know the answer to that.

You know I usually wait

until I surface for the third time.

Why can't I just admit that I can't swim?

And keep you, the Lifesaver,

with me at all times?

TERRY POWELL

That day when evening came, he said to his disciples, "Let us go over to the other side." A furious squall came up, and the waves broke over the boat, so that it was nearly swamped. Jesus was in the stern, sleeping on a cushion. The disciples

**woke him and said to him, "Teacher, don't you care if we
drown?" He got up, rebuked the wind and said to the waves,
"Quiet! Be still!" Then the wind died down and it was
completely calm. He said to his disciples, "Why are you so
afraid? Do you still have no faith?" They were terrified and
asked each other, "Who is this? Even the wind and the waves
obey him!"**

MARK 4:35, 37-41

Instead of going to God early
on—at the first hint of a problem, the first intimation of
depression, the first rush of red-hot anger—we too often wait until
the situation has escalated beyond our control. Then we reproach
God for not being more involved in our lives. The disciples grew
more and more fearful of the storm that had whipped up out of
nowhere. And with their fear grew resentment. Hadn't Jesus told
them to cross over to the other side? How could he sleep when they
were about to lose their lives at any moment? Their first statement
wasn't a request, it was an accusation: "Don't you even care?"
Though he was never asked to, Jesus calmed the storm. He also
exposed the root of the disciples' fear. They didn't believe he was
more powerful than what they were up against.

We often share the disciples' lack of faith. We don't really believe
God will work for our behalf, so we sweat it out alone until we are
in desperate need. We ought to become careful sailors, noting the
first wind shift or change in the sky, seeking immediate refuge. A
boat, after all, can capsize in a second.

*Dear God, thank you for your
immediate interest in my life.
May I not put off seeking your
help. Amen.*

GOD PRINTS

I.

You'd expect him to make himself known,

to appear at our party, you might say,

if God is really out there.

He wouldn't travel the cosmos incognito.

And if he is at all good,

interested in our questions and needs,

for sure he'd step out of

the shadows, identify himself,

and share his strategy for a better life. Wouldn't he have one,

after all,

if he were God?

Perhaps that's why religions

of all major name brands

have always figured

God would somehow let us in on his secrets.

You'd just expect him to. Maybe he would write a book.

There are hints that God is around.

He leaves footprints in nature

rather like a contractor

leaves neat seams in sidewalks.

"God was here."

It's scrawled like graffiti

in the face of canyons,

in the great galactic expanse of Andromeda,

in the gnarled bark of eucalyptus trees,

in the microscopic complexity of even

the simplest cells,

in the aerodynamics of honeybees.

Yet in spite of the evidence that says

God is here,

thousands of unanswered questions

beg for a more definitive word:

Why do bad people fare so well?

Why do mothers have to watch

their babies die from hunger and disease?

Why do earthquakes wipe out villages

and airplanes crash with friends

or family aboard?

And why can't I measure up

to even the minimal expectations

I have of myself? I've written a pop quiz

on philosophy, theology,

morals and ethics,

and egotistically

I expect God to pass it.

To put it bluntly:

If there is a God,

wouldn't he tell us

exactly what he's like;

and what he expects of us;

and why things aren't like they ought to be;

and what he intends to do about it?

But would he do it?

Would God even bother with my questions?

Would he write a book?

And if he did,

how would he do it?

The image of God

hunched over a typewriter

(rat-ta-tat-tat . . . bing!),

an open dictionary and thesaurus

at his side,

detracts somehow from my idea

of divine greatness.

If the vast stellar reaches

can't contain him

it seems odd,

incongruous,

to give him a final

or to assign him a term paper.

Or book.

I have a dilemma.

I am torn between expecting God

to be distant

(because he's so great)

and wanting him to be accessible.

I want to know he has spoken,

but I am almost afraid to hear him.

Because if he has shared his strategy for life,

and if he's answered my questions

(or chosen not to),

I am obligated to accept it.

If he's God.

I must acquiesce to his directions when he speaks

and accept his silence when he doesn't.

If he's made himself known,

if he's stepped from the shadows

and appeared at my party,

I have to welcome him,

if he's God.

And if he's written a book,

I ought to read it.

JIM LONG

The heavens declare the glory of God; the skies proclaim the work of his hands. Day after day they pour forth speech; night after night they display knowledge. There is no speech or language where their voice is not heard. Their voice goes out into all the earth, their words to the ends of the world. The law of the Lord is perfect, reviving the soul. The statutes of the Lord are trustworthy, making wise the simple. The precepts of the Lord are right, giving joy to the heart. The commands of the Lord are radiant, giving light to the eyes. The fear of the Lord is pure, enduring forever. The ordinances of the Lord are sure and altogether righteous. They are more precious than gold, than much pure gold; they are sweeter than honey, than honey from the comb. By keeping them is your servant warned; in keeping them there is great reward.

PSALM 19:1-4, 7-11

How can you come to know someone without meeting and talking face-to-face? You study what the person has written or created, and if the opportunity arises, you communicate in other ways—by corresponding, for instance. Searching for God is no different; we can look at the world around us; we can study his Word; we can learn to communicate with him. God can be known. But we need to look for him in the right places.

Creation points to God and displays his power and imagination, but clay and wheat and horseshoe crabs aren't God. Infants, sagging middle-aged adults, and grandparents are made in the image of God, but they aren't God in the flesh. The Bible is God's Word, but sixty-six books of ink and tissue-thin paper can't contain him. God offers us the possibility of coming to know him through all these things, and by communicating with him in prayer, but such knowledge requires patient work. Knowing and understanding another person is never easy.

Dear God, thank you for caring enough to make yourself known to man. Help me to know and understand you better. Amen.

GOD PRINTS

II.

Christians are curious people;

they are convinced that God has spoken.

He has, they say, stepped from the shadows

and shared his strategy for life.

In fact, Christians claim

that God has not only spoken,

but that he has eloquently and

definitively spoken.

He has, they say, told us what he's like;

what he expects of us;

why things aren't like they ought to be;

and what he intends to do about it.

He has, they say, written a book.

Not that he hunched over a typewriter,

but rather that he stepped up to his people

and whispered messages in their minds.

The unnerving thing about it is this:

That book, the Bible, often gives answers,

but almost as often it leaves me

wondering.

And it does so without apology—

as if it's God's prerogative

to withhold information from me

at his initiative.

Sometimes the book comforts me

and other times it makes me feel

intensely disturbed.

But something happens when I

accept the Bible on its own terms.

The demands of life aren't exactly reduced,

neither are the questions automatically settled.

What changes is my outlook.

I begin to realize

that this book of his

is not at all like other documents—

cold, dead type

on cold, dead pages.

Instead, there's something of

God's own life in it.

And it gives me that strange breed

of delirious hope that comes

from finally meeting God

and discovering he cared enough

to write a book.

JIM LONG

Blessed are they whose ways are blameless, who walk according to the law of the Lord. Blessed are they who keep his statutes and seek him with all their heart. They do nothing wrong; they walk in his ways. You have laid down precepts that are to be fully obeyed. Oh, that my ways were steadfast in obeying your decrees! Then I would not be put to shame when I consider all your commands. I will praise you with an upright heart as I learn your righteous laws. I will obey your decrees; do not utterly forsake me. How can a young man keep his way pure? By living according to your word. I seek you with all my heart; do not let me stray from your commands. I have hidden your word in my heart that I might not sin against you. Praise be to you, O Lord; teach me your decrees. With my lips I recount all the laws that come from your mouth. I rejoice in following your statutes as one rejoices in great riches. I meditate on your precepts and consider your ways. I delight in your decrees; I will not neglect your word.

PSALM 119:1-16

Can words change anyone's life? Can the Bible make a difference in the way a person thinks and lives? Probably not, if it's only a collection of stories, moralistic directives, and the history of a particular group of people.

But if the Bible is actually, somehow, God speaking to man, then it is a *living* voice, and we must listen. Even listening is not enough—some change in attitude or behavior must follow.

God knows how difficult it is for us to listen and take action; he's provided help. His Spirit teaches us from what we've heard and read, and God himself strengthens us to live in obedience. God hasn't told us to do the impossible all on our own.

Dear God, thank you for your presence, which continually reminds me to listen to you. Strengthen me, I pray, that I might be obedient to what I hear. Amen.

OLD PLOT

Lord,

Amazingly, you died for me:

the ultimate expression of love.

How easy it is for me to nod that off

in callousness.

I often feel, as I read about the cross,

as if I'm watching summer reruns . . .

where the plot is already known

and thus, somehow less than exciting.

Forgive me.

I guess what I need is not more goose bumps, or sadness

at your pain and sorrow;

I need to know the cost of your cross,

and how it brought me freedom and new life.

May these new thoughts move me . . .

not to tears . . .

but to toil,

an active living for you, who died for me.

LYNETTE ALEXANDER

You have forsaken your first love.
REVELATION 2:4

Because of his great love for us, God, who is rich in mercy, made us alive with Christ even when we were dead in transgressions—it is by grace you have been saved.

EPHESIANS 2:4, 5

The most overwhelming thing about love is its willingness to give of itself repeatedly. Think about how your parents loved you when, as a baby, you did not love them in return. You cried; you demanded food and attention; you gave nothing back to those who hovered over you, trying to anticipate your every need. It wasn't until you grew older and understood the value of love that you wanted to love your parents back.

Sacrificial love is the most powerful force on earth. People who have been loved love others in the same way. People who have seen love in action love others actively. People who have experienced love don't give up when feelings run low. People who know they are loved by God want to love others as he does. Consider how God's love for you is evident and you'll find it easier to love him and other people. Love stretches far beyond sentimentality—it gets to the heart of the matter in thought and action.

Dear God, thank you for your great love for me, love that is active even when I don't acknowledge it. May I love others with the love you've given me. Amen.

SEX . . . IS LIKE A GIFT WRAPPED IN BROWN PAPER

There's a beautiful gift inside this package.

    It's wrapped for protection,

    Tied for security.

    Stamped: "Fragile!" "Handle with Care!"

It's easy to loosen the strings,

    To let anyone tear away the wrapping,

    To give the gift without commitment—

    Offer it to the highest bidder,

    Or hand it out as the prize for a game.

There's a gift wrapped inside this brown paper.

    It's for keeps—not to be exchanged.

    No deposit. Nonreturnable.

    It's a surprise,

    A happy treat to be opened by the person

    To whom it's addressed,

    On the date marked "Forever."

RUTH SENTER

Let us behave decently, as in the daytime, not in orgies and drunkenness, not in sexual immorality and debauchery, not in dissension and jealousy. Rather, clothe yourselves with the Lord Jesus Christ, and do not think about how to gratify the desires of the sinful nature.

ROMANS 13:13

Do you not know that the wicked will not inherit the kingdom of God? Do not be deceived: Neither the sexually immoral nor idolaters nor adulterers nor male prostitutes nor homosexual offenders will inherit the kingdom of God . . .

Flee from sexual immorality. All other sins a man commits are outside his body, but he who sins sexually sins against his own body. Do you not know that your body is a temple of the Holy Spirit, who is in you, whom you have received from God? You are not your own; you were bought at a price. Therefore honor God with your body.

1 CORINTHIANS 6:9, 18-20

God allows for a wide range of opinion on many issues—political systems, fashion, art. But on some topics God has left little room for discussion—the value of human life, the worship of other gods, treatment of the poor. And sex. The Bible is not at all vague about sex.

In Genesis 2 we read that God gave the first man and woman to each other. The Song of Solomon talks descriptively about the beauty of sex, while Proverbs warns against the abuses of sex. In the New Testament, Jesus and Paul both spoke about sex and marriage. Again and again, sex is mentioned in the Bible. Why? Because it's a matter of such consequence that God has not left it to personal opinion. Two people coming together sexually join bodies and souls. And that union, no matter how careless or inappropriate, is not easily severed.

Dear God, thank you for creating me a sexual being. Help me to live with my sexuality according to your will. Amen.

TERRA INCOGNITA

God's plan for my life

often seems a mystery.

But so are

quadratic equations,

idiot savants,

the black dahlia,

pictures produced by sound,

the relative size of mathematical infinity.

Why should the mind of God

be any less of a mystery?

PAM JOHNSON

Who has understood the Spirit of the Lord, or instructed him as his counselor? Whom did the Lord consult to enlighten him, and who taught him the right way? Who was it that taught him knowledge or showed him the path of understanding?

ISAIAH 40:13, 14

Oh, the depth of the riches of the wisdom and knowledge of God! How unsearchable his judgments, and his paths beyond tracing out! "Who has known the mind of the Lord? Or who has been his counselor?"

ROMANS 11:33, 34

97

If it were up to you, how would you plan your life? Would what seems best for you now be best for you in the future? Would riches make you generous or would they turn you into a miser? Would personal success make you proud and aloof or humble and willing to help others?

We make plans—a challenging career, a loving husband or wife, a couple of kids. But throw in economic slumps, illnesses, family problems, personal crises, and our orderly plans become a maze. God's plans for us aren't so easily scrambled. He knows what we'll face in the future, and he knows how to get us through it. Even more, he uses the events and people in our lives to make us more like himself, to teach us who he is and to show us who we are. We'll never fully understand God's plans for us or how he'll work out those plans, but we can learn to trust him. We can let God be God.

Dear God, thank you for being in control of my future. Increase my trust in you and your plans for me. Amen.

WHY IS IT GOOD NEWS?

I.

What do doctors and police have in common?

They get to spread bad news.

Police ring the doorbell late at night. Somebody comes in a

bathrobe, sleepy-eyed, and awakens to bad news:

a loved one is dead.

Doctors tell people they're dying of cancer.

  Nobody likes to spread the bad news.

  Everybody likes to tell good news.

You and your best friend both got an A on the test?

Guess who goes racing to tell him?

  The first Christians called their message about Jesus the

Good News (translated: gospel).

The term was not thought up by a public-relations firm.

They were not trying to stick a pretty label on some nasty

medicine.

They called it Good News spontaneously,

all over the world.

  We still call it Good News,

but we act, sometimes, like it's bad news.

We're reluctant to tell about it.

("I know I ought to.")

The meetings we have, where we talk about the Good News,

can have all the joy of a morticians' convention.

The solution isn't, as some think,

to slap on a grin and make everybody clap hands together.

You don't make it good news by pretending.

When you're honest with yourself, the question remains:

what's so good about the Good News?

Good news:

somebody you always

wanted to know

is in love with you.

That somebody is God.

He loves you and will sacrifice anything to help you.

Being significant to God means more than being significant

even to your best friend.

A friend can give you sympathy, but a God-friend can give you

direction:

he knows everything.

A God-friend can give you power:

there's nothing he can't change.

(And that includes the parts of you that are still

bad news.)

TIM STAFFORD

For God so loved the world that he gave his one and only Son, that whoever believes in him shall not perish but have eternal life.

JOHN 3:16

I pray also that the eyes of your heart may be enlightened in order that you may know the hope to which he has called you, the riches of his glorious inheritance in the saints, and his incomparably great power for us who believe. That power is like the working of his mighty strength, which he exerted in Christ when he raised him from the dead.

EPHESIANS 1:18-20

No one can perfectly disguise fear; it wears a transparent mask. If you're afraid to go off the high dive, it will affect your performance. You may eventually step up and off the platform, but your entry will be awkward. If you're afraid to talk about yourself—who you are and what you believe—your speech and actions will tell on you.

The opposite of fear is confidence. And confidence also shows. A person who is convinced of what he or she believes may not have all the answers, but he or she isn't afraid of the questions. The convinced person's faith lies in the subject at hand, not in his or her personal abilities. If the gospel of Jesus Christ has made a difference in your life, if you've recognized your need for God and have experienced his meeting of that need, your confidence in him is bound to show. There will be no need for masks as the transparent conviction of your faith shines through.

Dear God, fill me with confidence in you, and help others to see the reality of my faith. Amen.

WHY IS IT GOOD NEWS?

II.

Good news:

you're going

somewhere.

Before this, all you were headed toward

was a tombstone.

Maybe you'd make a lot of money.

Maybe you'd do great things.

But in a few years, who'd know? Who'd care?

Good news: that big cold universe is home

for a God who handcrafted it.

He has plans for you: he wants you to

participate in something that really matters:

something the earth was

created for, something that will last forever.

You're a key person in his eyes.

Good news:

life is fair.

Some say the only thing that counts is whether you

make yourself happy with success, with money,

with admirers, with sex, with whatever it is you're after.

No one else matters.

You only answer to yourself.

That's bad news,

because it means the cheaters and rapists

and muggers get exactly what they were after,

so long as they don't get caught.

And the mean-mouthed, the ugly-minded, the

utterly selfish come out even better, because

there's no law against their crimes.

Meanwhile those who love,

who sacrifice to feed the hungry,

who care about people too abused to care about

themselves (old people, beaten children, mentally disturbed,

and those too low on hope to ever pull themselves up),

get nothing.

And when you struggle to pray, to be kind, to love your

neighbor—you get nothing.

Virtue is its own reward—

the only reward.

But . . . there is good news about the future:

God is in control, and someday he will give rewards for love,

and rewards for selfishness too.

TIM STAFFORD

When Jesus spoke again to the people, he said, "I am the light of the world. Whoever follows me will never walk in darkness, but will have the light of life."

JOHN 8:12

The eyes of the Lord are everywhere, keeping watch on the wicked and the good.

PROVERBS 15:3

Serve wholeheartedly, as if you were serving the Lord, not men, because you know that the Lord will reward everyone for whatever good he does.

EPHESIANS 6:7, 8

Sometimes life seems like a big joke. Oh, it's OK for you and me, but not for the Ethiopian child dying because there isn't enough food. Not for the homeless woman sleeping in doorways and under city park trees. Not for the teenager unable to escape inner-city gangs and violence.

Christians know that God is fully aware of what's going on in the world, and that he wants it to change. God cared so much that he placed his own Son in the middle of the human situation, so mankind could have access to the only power capable of overcoming evil and injustice. Christians living out the good news of Jesus Christ are God's agents of change. Their activities make life seem less like a joke and more like God intended it to be for all people. And there is a benefit for the doers as well: their work is not unnoticed by God.

Dear God, encourage me to bring about change wherever I am, that your kingdom may be established on earth. Help me live out the good news of your salvation for mankind. Amen.

THE ARTIST BEHIND SISTER NATURE

I saw a sequoia once,
  a thirty-story giant.
I felt dwarfed, hushed . . . almost cold,
Until two irreverent squirrels appeared
    chasing tails around the mammoth trunk,
    oblivious.
I looked closer and saw nature's happy face.

Drunk with her autumn scent,
    I tried to worship nature once
    but failed.
A sequoia is awesome . . .
    but how do you worship a hurricane?
    rats' teeth?
    a plague?

No, nature, you're not our sacred Mother!
    You're our Sister.
You offer up a jolting mix
    of butterflies and gnats,
    swans and volcanoes.
Inviting yet vicious, you exist apart,
    you're created, like us—
    to frolic with and picnic in

and sometimes wrestle. . . .

A boy who builds a tree house

is closer to you, Sister,

than a man who carves an idol.

Squinting, I've seen your trees as paintings:

an Impressionist ironwood

a Renaissance sequoia

an abstract eucalyptus.

Long before man learned to paint

our Maker planted masterpieces,

delicate brushstrokes of tinted bark.

I wonder what delight God must have felt.

He could have left mere engineering marvels,

hulking shapes of steel–smooth wood.

Instead He sketched in lines and shadows.

He gave grooves and knots,

each tree a face.

You toss us many moods, Sister Nature.

The mossy, spidery mist of a rain forest,

the irrepressible cheeriness of spring,

the steamy pine scent of summer.

When I'm with you, though,

I mainly feel delight,

the thrill of a fellow creation,

celebrating God's artistry.

I saw you, Sister, in a giant cypress,

still winter-bare and gray

in a Southern swamp.

I climbed it

and looked at the worm tracks

on its bark

and sniffed its spongy wetness

and spotted a squirrel's nest

too far out to reach,

and a clump of mistletoe too high.

I could have taken part of a branch home,

to shape into a picture frame.

Or I could have scarred my name

across the tree's trunk.

Instead, I left it—

because it fit.

It had a place.

You're my Sister, nature,

and I love you for your temper

(even though I fear it)

as well as for your playfulness.

I love you because you remind me

of our Maker,

who painted us both with

   intricate detail,

but respected us enough to let us fit,

in place,

with Him.

PHILIP YANCEY

To whom, then, will you compare God? What image will you compare him to? Do you not know? Have you not heard? Has it not been told you from the beginning? Have you not understood since the earth was founded? He sits enthroned above the circle of the earth, and its people are like grasshoppers. He stretches out the heavens like a canopy, and spreads them out like a tent to live in.

"To whom will you compare me? Or who is my equal?" says the Holy One. Lift your eyes and look to the heavens: Who created all these? He who brings out the starry host one by one, and calls them each by name. Because of his great power and mighty strength, not one of them is missing. Do you not know? Have you not heard? The Lord is the everlasting God, the Creator of the ends of the earth.

ISAIAH 40:18, 21, 22, 25, 26, 28

When was the last time you noticed, really noticed, how intricate the natural world is? Do you have to see something as spectacular as the Rockies before you give creation a thought? When did you last watch a line of ants marching across a city sidewalk, or offer a prayer of thanks for the fresh water running from a park fountain? Are you not awed at the way thunderstorms roll in out of nowhere on summer afternoons?

We are plainly instructed: Do not worship nature; worship its

Creator. But we are not to ignore nature, or even take a complacent attitude toward it, for God also instructed us to care for his creation. God created the natural world first, solely for his delight. And then God created mankind and gave him a place within nature. It's God's plan that we be active observers and participants in the good things he created.

Dear God, thank you for the beauty and mighty power of nature. May I be a faithful steward of it—in thought and action. Amen.

FACES OF ME

I am not really myself.

I am someone else.

When others talk with me

They are talking to a stranger.

I am kept hidden away,

Safe from discovery or attack

Behind the cover of my masks.

Each day,

Sometimes knowingly, sometimes not,

As I sift through my closet,

Choosing which clothes to wear,

I also search my mental mask menagerie,

Carefully selecting the image I want to project.

Like an actor,

I have learned to portray many roles,

Many faces,

Many moods.

And I use a different mask for each.

Each mask represents

The me I would like to be.

I put on a mask of happiness because

I sincerely want to be happy;

I wear the socialite mask because

I want to have fun,

The self-sufficiency mask because

I truly want to take charge of my life.

Something peculiar happens, however,

As I continue wearing these masks.

They begin to feel too comfortable,

Natural,

Necessary.

As I get used to my masks,

I begin to believe they might really be me.

Meanwhile, my true self lies

Dormant,

Forgotten.

Like a brick wall, the masks confine me,

Isolate me,

Hide me from other people.

When I don the mask of conformity

I'm really broadcasting my own lack of

   identity.

When I wear the mask of confidence,

Refusing to admit weakness, mistakes or hurt,

I'm telegraphing my own insecurity.

I have other masks:

The mask of superiority

To stare down inferior feelings

I detect in others

And in myself;

The clown or the rowdy masks

To gain the attention I can't obtain otherwise;

The "together" mask

To hide all my rough edges;

The mask of love

To disguise an overly selfish relationship;

Even the mask of spirituality

To silence all questions about my status before

   God.

What should I do with all my masks?

If indeed I want to be myself

Rather than someone else,

I must remove them,

Peel them off,

Cut them away like a plaster cast.

Some of the worthless masks I will trample to pieces.

Others I will display on my bedroom wall

To remind me of the person I'd like to be,

But am not yet.

Ultimately, I won't need masks;

Instead,

I'll show others the living person behind them:

An authentic human being—

Someone who's not perfect, but who wants to grow.

Only when I open myself to other people

will I see myself clearly.

And only when I take off the masks

Will I be truly free.

VERNE BECKER

O Lord, you have searched me and you know me. You know when I sit and when I rise; you perceive my thoughts from afar. You discern my going out and my lying down; you are familiar with all my ways. Where can I go from your Spirit? Where can I flee from your presence? If I say, "Surely the darkness will hide me and the light become night around me," even the darkness will not be dark to you; the night will shine like the day, for darkness is as light to you. Search me, O God, and know my heart.

PSALM 139:1-3, 7, 11, 12, 23

Wearing masks is a way of protecting ourselves. If we act and look like everyone else, no one will notice our differences. The problem: With everyone wearing masks, it becomes impossible to discern who is real and who isn't.

It takes a person of character to put aside his or her masks. And it takes a person of courage, because authenticity stands out. Unmasked people tell you what they think. If they don't like a style, they don't go with it. If they are just as happy at home on Friday nights as they are standing around at parties, they just say, "No thanks." It's easy and refreshing to be around people who have taken off their masks. They make us want to take off ours.

Dear God, help me put aside my many masks and put on my authenticity. Amen.

SOMETIMES I FEEL LIKE A BLIND CAVE FISH

Slippery-pink, swimming your life away

    deep in the belly of a cave.

Rather secure, isn't it?

You know each limestone dimple

    and merrily scoot around,

        testing the limits of your blindness.

Eyeless,

    you don't even dart away

    when I shine my flashlight.

Those cracks and jagged peaks you memorize—

    you can't see their beauty.

The water-drip of centuries sculpted them as

    an underground act of worship.

But you nudge them, unseeing.

I could shine a light on them for you, fish,

    if you had eyes.

And I could tell you of a larger world

    outside . . .

    new colors—turquoise and violet and scarlet—

    and light so dazzling this flashlight beam

    would disappear.

Would you care, blind fish?

Would you beg for eyes and a new body
> to explore this new dimension?
Or would you scurry to the safety of your
> shapeless playground, thinking me crazy
> for inventing strange words like "light"?

Poor fish, you're too much like me.
I love the blinders that shield me from
> revealing, demanding,
> escape-proof light.
I prefer stumbling to searching
> for that light.

Some say one Man split history with
> words like
> "I am the light,"
> "I'll pull you from the darkness,"
> "Follow me."
He banished the darkness of his burial cave.
See him, they say,
> and by him you can see.

PHILIP YANCEY

*I am the light of the world. Whoever follows me will never
walk in darkness, but will have the light of life.*
JOHN 8:12

But everything exposed by the light becomes visible, for it is light that makes everything visible. This is why it is said: "Wake up, O sleeper, rise from the dead, and Christ will shine on you."

EPHESIANS 5:13, 14

Walk out into the sunshine after being in a dark room and your eyes will hurt. Light is painful when you're not used to it. But without light, you can't see anything. No form. No color. No detail.

Christ is the Light of the World, and he starts by being the light of individual men and women. Bearing Christ's light can be painful, as your personal darkness—jealousy, greed, bitterness, pride—is exposed. But Christ's light at work within you will purify and heal and invigorate and add color to your life, and you'll eventually begin to see with God's sight. Not allowing Christ to pierce your life with the light of his presence is to remain in darkness, where you'll eventually lose the ability to see yourself for who you really are.

Dear God, please show me who I am by the light of your presence, that I may no longer walk in darkness. Amen.

WORD CHECK

I don't always mean what I say.

I don't always say what I mean.

Sometimes I say what I think will make you like me:

something

witty

clever

cute

entertaining.

Sometimes I say what will keep me out of trouble:

bend the truth

exaggerate

halve the facts.

Sometimes I say what will make me look good:

wow 'em with words

compliment

praise

sound

pious

poised

and put together.

About my words, Lord:

Please check them out for truth.

RUTH SENTER

Set a guard over my mouth, O Lord; keep watch over the door of my lips.

PSALM 141:3

The tongue is a small part of the body, but it makes great boasts. Consider what a great forest is set on fire by a small spark. With the tongue we praise our Lord and Father, and with it we curse men, who have been made in God's likeness. Out of the same mouth come praise and cursing. My brothers, this should not be.

JAMES 3:5, 9, 10

You'd think that controlling our tongues would be a cinch. (We control other, much larger parts of our bodies with relative ease.) And we occasionally fool ourselves into thinking that our tongues are under control, until we get mad at a sister for snooping in our things or an umpire for making a bad call. Then, without thinking and without coaxing, our tongues take over: words fly, venting our frustration and anger, alienating us from friends and family. But it's not only in bad times that we lose control. With our tongues we put others down and praise ourselves. We dish out compliments for the sake of gaining attention. We speak insincerely.

Why can't we manage what we say and how we say it? Because our tongues are the mouthpiece of our hearts. Whatever we are on the inside—good or bad—is expressed in our words. Instead of asking God first to change our tongues, we should ask him to change our hearts. We'll speak with gentleness and patience and genuineness and understanding when our hearts are that way. It's the inside person we most need to place under God's control.

Dear God, forgive me for the lack of control I have over what I think and feel, and what I say. Change me on the inside, that I may be changed on the outside. Amen.

OLYMPIAN

Father,

We run so fast to inch forward,

  when we could let you power our legs.

We leap at hurdles,

  when we could make them shorter.

We strain to vault the bar,

  when we could fly.

We flail against the crashing waves,

  when we could walk on the water,

  if only we looked to you in faith.

PAM JOHNSON

Do you not know that in a race all the runners run, but only one gets the prize? Run in such a way as to get the prize. Everyone who competes in the games goes into strict training. They do it to get a crown that will not last; but we do it to get a crown that will last forever.

1 CORINTHIANS 9:24, 25

Even youths grow tired and weary, and young men stumble and fall; but those who hope in the Lord will renew their strength. They will soar on wings like eagles; they will run and not grow weary, they will walk and not be faint.

ISAIAH 40:30, 31

The race requires endurance and speed. Run too fast, too hard, and you'll never make it; you'll burn out before the finish line. Run with too little commitment, and you'll drop out as others begin to pass you by. Like all runners, you need to temper your pace with the reality of your condition. A person in poor physical shape doesn't suddenly start running marathons. He or she builds up to it with consistent practice. And practice is hard work: it's doing the same thing again and again. In addition to practice, runners eat the right kinds of food, get enough rest, and keep their goals constantly in mind.

The race you've entered as a Christian demands no less of you. Your training is costly—time spent with God in daily Bible study and prayer, the development of a life-style that conforms to God's expectations, the high goal of having God's approval in every area of your life. Don't be discouraged if you feel that you're not yet where you want to be as a Christian. But don't give up, either. Instead of going it alone, ask Christian friends to run with you. Look for areas where you can improve and ways to grow stronger, but also look at how far you've progressed. A runner doesn't give up because he has an off day on the track. Neither should you.

Dear God, thank you for running the race with me. Pick me up when I fall, and set me on the course when I stray. May the rewards of finishing the race be ever before me. Amen.

NO WORDS

God,

   You're beyond me.

I can't tell

   how wonderful you are.

I can't find

   adjectives

   dazzling or

   immense enough.

How does one describe total goodness?

There are no words

   to comprehend

   or circumscribe

Your greatness.

NANCY SPIEGELBERG

Now to the King eternal, immortal, invisible, the only God, be honor and glory for ever and ever. Amen.
1 TIMOTHY 1:17

The trumpeters and singers joined in unison, as with one voice, to give praise and thanks to the Lord. Accompanied by trumpets, cymbals and other instruments, they raised their voices in praise to the Lord and sang: "He is good; his love endures forever."
2 CHRONICLES 5:13

It's a paradox—we are created in God's image, thus we are something like him. Yet, we are nothing like him. God is the epitome, the definition of everything that we can only begin to be: good, just, righteous, patient, kind, sacrificial, holy.

We can begin to grow like him only when we recognize how wonderful he is, how utterly unlike us in his perfection, and praise him for it.

Dear God, forgive me for wanting to bring you down to my size. Work within me, that my character may be a truer reflection of yours. Amen.

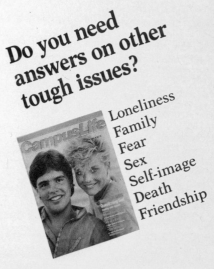

CAMPUS LIFE is the largest, most colorful Christian youth magazine in the world. Month after month, CAMPUS LIFE helps thousands of teens keep their faith intact in a world falling apart. Like a trusted friend, it provides solid counsel, encouragement and just plain fun.

☐ Please send me a full year (10 issues) of CAMPUS LIFE for only $11.95—40% off the cover price.

☐ Payment enclosed
☐ Please bill me

Name _____

Address _____

City _____ State ___ Zip _____

Outside U.S. prices for one year: $14.95 U.S. funds; $19.00 Canadian funds. Please allow 6 weeks for delivery of first issue.

Do you need answers on other tough issues?

Loneliness
Family
Fear
Sex
Self-image
Death
Friendship

E6JCLBKN

BUSINESS REPLY MAIL

FIRST CLASS   PERMIT NO. 1596   WHEATON, IL

POSTAGE WILL BE PAID BY ADDRESSEE

CAMPUS LIFE
Subscription Service
465 Gundersen Dr.
Carol Stream, IL 60188

BUSINESS REPLY MAIL

FIRST CLASS   PERMIT NO. 1596   WHEATON, IL

POSTAGE WILL BE PAID BY ADDRESSEE

CAMPUS LIFE
Subscription Service
465 Gundersen Dr.
Carol Stream, IL 60188

MERRY-GO-ROUND

Don't

    let me ride

    a gaudy

merry-go-round

    Christian experience:

Up-and-down

Round-and-round

    noisy

    fun

    set to music,

Never really getting

    anywhere

    but sadly back

    to where

    I first

    got on.

NANCY SPIEGELBERG

And this is my prayer: that your love may abound more and more in knowledge and depth of insight, so that you may be able to discern what is best and may be pure and blameless until the day of Christ, filled with the fruit of righteousness that comes through Jesus Christ—to the glory and praise of God.

PHILIPPIANS 1:9-11

And we, who with unveiled faces all reflect the Lord's glory, are being transformed into his likeness with ever-increasing glory, which comes from the Lord, who is the Spirit.

2 CORINTHIANS 3:18

It's natural to want our Christian experience to be one of constant excitement, good feelings, and high emotion. But God has not called us to live in a carnival-like world. The ups and downs of everyday life, the pains and joys of friendship and love, the tragedies that touch families and communities are as much a part of a Christian's life as anyone's.

God hasn't placed us on a carefree merry-go-round. But he has promised that our lives will be richer with his presence and peace as we grow closer to him. He has promised to move us ahead in our relationships with him, until we are more perfectly conformed to his image. Merry-go-rounds eventually stop. God wants you to move ahead forever. He offers an authentic ride for all takers. And it never ends.

Dear God, forgive me for wanting the easy, fun way as a Christian. Move me ahead in your own way and time, I pray. Amen.

O COMMON NIGHT

He opened a window in the sky

and invited me to peer through it,

to catch even a faint glimpse

of what was going on,

what he was trying to do.

I expected a display

of unquestionable supremacy.

But what did I find?

A faint breeze

of roundabout power.

Everything

was so contradictory

to my way of thinking,

my way of doing things.

If he had retained his power

and an authoritative bearing . . .

made a grandiose entry,

asserted himself,

demanded that I acquiesce,

fortified his demands

with a show of blazing power . . .

If he had come flaunting

his obvious mastery, of course,

I would bend in submission.

Instead,

his coming was disgustingly commonplace.

He was,

at the heart of things,

far too normal

to command my admiration.

A peasant girl in her teens

for a mother.

A common laborer from a hick town

for a father.

And controversy over his legitimacy

buzzing through the village grapevine.

And yet there was a twist

to his commonness.

He defied categories.

The labels didn't stick.

He peeled them off,

insisting that I find another explanation.

He would not permit me to dismiss him

as a merely common,

ordinary,

man.

He made bizarre, outrageous claims,

unflinchingly.

"Before Abraham was,

I am."

"I and the Father

are one."

"I am the way,

and the truth,

and the life.

No man comes to God the Father

except through me."

Such brazen egotism!

And yet . . .

A sick man stands,

his hand withered,

and he waits for mercy.

For healing.

For healing?

It's one of those moments

you can never fully describe

afterward.

As if earth and heaven

were poised,

waiting for the inevitable.

Waiting for mercy.

For something more.

Did I question

his ability and willingness to heal?

Or merely the propriety

of practicing his supernatural medicine

on a sacred day?

JIM LONG

When Jesus came to the region of Caesarea Philippi, he asked his disciples, "Who do people say the Son of Man is?" They replied, "Some say John the Baptist; others say Elijah; and still others, Jeremiah or one of the prophets." "But what about you?" he asked. "Who do you say I am?" Simon Peter answered, "You are the Christ, the Son of the living God."

MATTHEW 16:13-16

I am the resurrection and the life. He who believes in me will live, even though he dies; and whoever lives and believes in me will never die. Do you believe this?

JOHN 11:25, 26

Christ's story isn't your typical kingly chronicle. In picture books, and sometimes in real life, royalty who have been wrongly subjected to poverty and abuse get their crowns and kingdoms in the end. Not so for Christ. He got a cross. But he never changed his declaration of kingship: Before he died he said his kingdom would have no end. To take him at his word means he is still king today.

Christ's contemporaries, the people who greeted him on the streets and warily critiqued his miracles, had to decide what they thought of the self-proclaimed Messiah. They followed him around to be sure they were in on the latest. They gossiped about him and discounted what they witnessed. But after awhile, some came to believe what he said of himself. Thousands of years later, we must still decide what we think of Christ. For if he is indeed king, then he has claim to our allegiance.

Dear God, thank you for the kingship of your Son. Might I bring honor to his name. Amen.

THE STORM INSIDE

Sometimes I let my emotions

paint my picture of God.

When I am depressed,

my image of God is microscopic,

a small blotch of blue paint

smeared in a tiny corner

of a giant canvas.

When I am angry,

my picture of God is ugly—

a hideous monster

using circumstances to devour me.

But when things are going well

and my joy spins with good times,

God seems kind

and I paint him with a smile.

Is he really as uneven

as my roller-coaster emotions?

Sometimes

I put the blame where it belongs.

God doesn't change—he can't.

The problem is with me.

I am the one who gets frustrated.

How can I blame God?

I am the one who is mad

and who lets my anger seethe.

I try to be so consistent—

to present a together front.

Then some unexpected conflict comes,

some unforeseen hassle,

and I lose it.

My weakness is out in the open.

And what does that prove?

The problem is not with God

but with me.

Maybe there's some point

to my changing moods.

Maybe there are natural highs

and recurring lows.

The shifting emotional tides

are, perhaps, normal.

But normal or not,

at times I just feel cruddy.

And when I do,

everything seems cruddy.

My emotions are a storm.

I struggle against them,

trying to understand them,

control them.

But they are unpredictable

and their intensity

overwhelms me.

But when my emotions run counter to reason,

do I have to follow them?

Can't I accept them,

affirm them,

express them,

vent them,

without letting them carry me

where I do not want to go?

God made me with this vivid spectrum

of emotion.

Even the stark and barren feelings

have their place in his blueprint.

He made me like him:

able to care,

to feel pain and joy

as he feels pain and joy,

to weep and laugh

as he weeps and laughs.

Yet in him I see balance and control—

emotion directed by reason

and tempered with self-sacrificing concern,

even for those who wrong him.

In this I see an answer

to my runaway emotions.

And a clear image of God

waiting to be painted.

JIM LONG

In the beginning you laid the foundations of the earth, and the heavens are the work of your hands. They will perish, but you remain; they will all wear out like a garment. Like clothing you will change them and they will be discarded. But you remain the same, and your years will never end.

PSALM 102:25-27

I the Lord do not change.

MALACHI 3:6

God created us to respond to life, and one way we respond is through our emotions. We respond to events in life that bring good things to us. We respond to changes in life that aren't so good. Because we are emotional beings, we respond to each other; our emotions bond us in humanity with people whom we don't even know.

To not have a full range of emotions would render us less like God and more like computers. True, God isn't depressed by three days of rain, but he understands depression. And insecurity. And fear. Yet God doesn't desire that our emotions run our lives. For our emotions to gain the upper hand is to risk losing the power to think and reason and understand and accept. Our emotions should help flesh out our perspective of the world, not dominate it.

Dear God, thank you for the wide range of feelings I am capable of experiencing. Help me to be no more and no less influenced by my emotions than is pleasing to you. Amen.

STIFF-CRUSHED-DEAD

He always wanted to explain things.

    But no one cared.

So he drew.

Sometimes he would draw and it wasn't anything.

He wanted to carve it in stone

    or write it in the sky.

And it would be only him and the sky

    and the thing inside him that needed saying.

It was after that he drew a picture.

It was a beautiful picture.

He kept it under his pillow

    and would let no one see it.

And it was all of him.

He would look at it every night

    and think about it.

When it was dark, and his eyes were closed,

    he could still see it.

When he started school he brought it with him

    like a friend.

It was funny about school.

He sat in a square brown desk,

    like all the other square brown desks.

And his room was a square brown room.

like all the other rooms.

And it was tight and close.

And stiff.

He hated to hold the pencil and chalk,

With his arm stiff and his feet flat on the floor.

Stiff.

With the teacher watching and watching.

The teacher came and spoke to him.

She told him to wear a tie like all the other boys.

He said he didn't like them.

And she said it didn't matter!

After that they drew.

And he drew all yellow and it was the way he felt
   about morning.

And it was beautiful.

The teacher came and smiled at him.

"What's this?" she said. "Why don't you draw
   something like Ken's drawing? Isn't that
   beautiful?"

After that his mother bought him a tie.

And he always drew airplanes
   and rocket ships like everyone else.

And he threw the old picture away.

And when he lay alone looking at the sky,

it was big and blue and full of everything.

But he wasn't anymore.

He was square inside,

and brown.

And his hands were stiff.

And he was like everyone else.

And the thing inside him that needed saying

didn't need saying anymore.

It had stopped pushing.

It was crushed.

Stiff.

Like everything else.

This poem was handed in to a teacher in Regina, Saskatchewan, by a student. He committed suicide a few weeks later.

You, my brothers, were called to be free. But do not use your freedom to indulge the sinful nature; rather, serve one another in love. The entire law is summed up in a single command: "Love your neighbor as yourself." If you keep on biting and devouring each other, watch out or you will be destroyed by each other.

GALATIANS 5:13–15

Sometimes we kill people with our expectations. We only see them as we want to see them, not as they really are. Yet God has given each man and woman particular gifts to be developed and used; he never planned for humanity to be a monolithic mass. Creation shows that God likes diversity.

It's easy to peg people, to put them into boxes that determine how we think they should act, what we think they should study, what hobbies we think they should enjoy. We pride ourselves in thinking how ultimately right and correct we are, but our expectations are only man-made. We can learn something from the Creator of all life. He made each one different, and called it good.

Dear God, forgive me for acting as though I am responsible for directing other people's lives. May I enjoy the differences of individuals, as you do. Amen.

ALIVE AGAIN

Universe and every universe beyond,

spin and blaze,

whirl and dance,

leap and laugh

as never before.

It's happened.

It's new.

It's here.

The liberation.

The victory.

The new creation.

Christ has smashed death.

He has liberated the world.

He has freed the universe.

You and I and everything

are free again,

new again,

alive again.

Let's have a festival

and follow Him across the skies,

through the flames of heaven

and back down every alley of our town.

There, let's have Him come

to liberate our city,

clean up the mess

and start all over again.

You conquered.

Keep on fighting through us.

You arose.

Keep on rising in us.

You celebrated.

Keep on celebrating with us.

You happen.

You are new.

You are here.

Lord of the winds

and fires of earth,

before we turn cold and hard

and blunt and brittle with apathy,

agitate our spirits.

Feed us with the flames

of love and laughter

that burn for us in others.

Surprise them again.

Surprise us again.

Surprise the earth again

by rising

and rising

within our bodies,

within our faith.

We ask because we can,

thanks to You,

Spirit–God–Man.

NORMAN HABEL

We were therefore buried with him through baptism into death in order that, just as Christ was raised from the dead through the glory of the Father, we too may live a new life. If we have been united with him in his death, we will certainly also be united with him in his resurrection.

ROMANS 6:4, 5

Since, then, you have been raised with Christ, set your hearts on things above, where Christ is seated at the right hand of God. Set your minds on things above, not on earthly things. For you died, and your life is now hidden with Christ in God. When Christ, who is your life, appears, then you also will appear with him in glory.

COLOSSIANS 3:1-4

We too easily forget the authentic power of the Christ who lives within us. He died for our sins and conquered once and for all the dark evilness of death. No one else has ever done that, yet we shrug it off as though defeating death is commonplace. He caused crippled people to leap and turned well water into quality wine, and he says we have access to the same power if we want it. Yet we mumble something about not being too charismatic. He sets men and women free today; he transforms callous men into gentle men. He gives bitter women back their hearts. He sets confused youths in the right direction. Yet we doubt his ability to work in our lives, to transform us into people who please him.

The very same Christ we read about in the Bible and occasionally pray to is alive in power and glory. He is alive in Christians. He is alive in his church. He is alive wherever there is life and joy and goodness. But the place he most wants to be alive is in you. To worship the risen Christ is to be alive with his presence.

Dear God, be as real to me now as you were to the people I read about in the Bible. May your presence in my life fill me with your character. Amen.

FAITH

A tiny speck.

A dot of next-to-nothingness.

A mustard seed.

Yet—

Deftly nurture

With soil and sun and rain,

And it will gain

Life.

Reaching down for sustenance.

Reaching up for air and sunshine.

Green leaves and yellow blossoms,

A thousand times a thousand

Larger than it was.

How can this be?

The miracle eludes us

But it is. It is. It is!

ROBERTA STROTKAMP

As Jesus went on from there, two blind men followed him, calling out, "Have mercy on us, Son of David!" When he had gone indoors, the blind men came to him, and he asked them, "Do you believe that I am able to do this?" "Yes, Lord," they replied. Then he touched their eyes and said, "According to your faith will it be done to you."

MATTHEW 9:27-29

And without faith it is impossible to please God, because anyone who comes to him must believe that he exists and that he rewards those who earnestly seek him.

HEBREWS 11:6

Faith is the lifeblood of Christianity. Faith was required of the Old Testament patriarchs who believed that God would send a better way. Faith was required of Jesus' contemporaries who were faced with his claims. Faith is required of us today. The remarkable thing about faith is not that God requires it, but that he'll give it to you, and that he'll increase it.

A person of great faith has nothing to pride himself in since God gave it to him in the first place. A person struggling with her faith need only ask God to meet her where she is. Sometimes the best anyone can say is, "Lord, I want a greater faith. Please do for me what I can't do for myself." Just as the rain and soil nurture seeds planted in the ground, producing all kinds of crops, God nurtures those who desire to see their faith grow. Through contact with other believers, through study and prayer, and by anticipating and meeting their needs, God grows his people into a steadfast faith. The crop he produces is unshakable.

Dear God, I often think that my faith is so very weak. Please work within me to strengthen it, to assure me of your power and reality. Thank you. Amen.

ONE OF THESE NIGHTS, GOD

I keep thinking, Lord,

how I should pray—

really pray.

Not just mumble some "Bless 'ems"

before I drop off to sleep.

I should really pray.

And I plan to do it

later,

after I watch TV,

after I take a bath.

But—

then it's too late, again.

I'm just too tired.

But one of these nights, boy,

I'm really gonna pray.

LOIS BREINER

One day Jesus was praying in a certain place. When he finished, one of his disciples said to him, "Lord, teach us to pray."

LUKE 11:1

And when you pray, do not keep on babbling like pagans, for they think they will be heard because of their many words.

MATTHEW 6:7

You wouldn't go for days or weeks without talking to your best friend. Why? Because you would feel out of touch with that person, and you'd know your friend would be out of touch with you. Because you need the consistent support and understanding a best friend can offer. Because conversation with a best friend is something you look forward to.

Maybe you should think of God more as a friend. Throw out the prayer formulas and talk with him as you would another person. Tell God how you feel about life, about him, about who you are. Explain your fears and dreams. Ask God to be real to you as you pray. Honesty in conversation binds people together; it gets beyond the pretended self to the real self. Likewise, honesty in prayer will bind your heart to God.

Dear God, may time spent with you in prayer become as vital to me as time spent talking with my friends. Amen.

NO MATTER WHAT

I.

I've failed again. I thought it would be different this time;

I was determined to act the way I wanted,

and that thought made me glad.

Now I'm low.

I want to pick myself up and forget it,

to tell myself,

"So what, you're only human.

You'll do better next time."

   But will I?

Will I do better next time?

If I get this right, I'll fail at something else.

   Everywhere I look,

I find people wanting more of me than I'm able to give.

There's no escaping it—

life bristles with rules and regulations and expectations.

Sit up straight and don't talk back.

Study first, then play.

Did you clean your room?

What were you doing out so late?

And if you think you have to measure up

in order to be worth anything,

you may as well admit it:

You're worthless.

Worthless.

What does Jesus have to do with us?

Most of my friends think he's just more rules.

Good rules, sure:

"Love your neighbor."

"Love God."

But good rules or bad rules,

what's the difference if I don't measure up?

   But my friends are wrong this time.

What Jesus is really about, most of all,

is forgiveness and love.

No matter what.

My parents have rules, and teachers have rules,

and the police have rules.

I hate the way my parents

always remind me when I'm wrong.

I wish I were the type who kept rules

all the time, without hassles.

   Yesterday I yelled at my sister,

fighting over what to watch on TV. And Mom

yelled at me. I yelled back, and went outside

to watch the sky. I got cold and went

back in. Watching my sister's show,

I felt like an outcast. I'd failed.

But this is when God loves me the most.

He loves me no matter what.

TIM STAFFORD

I do not understand what I do. For what I want to do I do not do, but what I hate I do. I know that nothing good lives in me, that is, in my sinful nature. For I have the desire to do what is good, but I cannot carry it out. What a wretched man I am! Who will rescue me from this body of death? Thanks be to God—through Jesus Christ our Lord!

ROMANS 7:15, 18, 24, 25

For it is by grace you have been saved, through faith—and this not from yourselves, it is the gift of God—not by works, so that no one can boast.

EPHESIANS 2:8, 9

One of the hardest things any person can do is say, "I'm sorry. Please forgive me." But that is what Christians are called upon to do regularly. Every day of our lives we fail God and man by entertaining inappropriate thoughts, by putting our personal interests above those of others, by making hasty judgments . . . our personal lists are endless. Yet we hesitate to ask forgiveness because we don't like to admit how imperfect we are. Perhaps we fear losing God's approval.

It is not God's desire that we view seeking forgiveness as an act of self-flagellation. Instead, it is to remind us of who we are and of all that Christ has done for us. It is, in many ways, a joyous act, for to be forgiven is to be restored to a right relationship with God and others. Yet to ask forgiveness will cost our pride; only the guilty recognize personal insufficiencies. When we go to God, confessing our sin and asking for his forgiveness, we acknowledge our need for his love and acceptance. At such times we will not find that he fails us.

Dear God, thank you for loving me no matter how much I disappoint you. And thank you for always being ready to forgive me. Amen.

NO MATTER WHAT

II.

Go to church on Sunday.

Love God all the time, more and more and more.

Have you read your Bible?

I haven't read the Bible all week.

Last week I did,

but it can't have done me much good.

I can't even remember where I was reading from.

And though I tried at times to pray to God,

my words didn't mean anything . . .

I started thinking about a test.

And I felt as if God were frowning on me,

from up high,

so distant his unhappy face was just a dot.

   I felt he couldn't be close to me.

But I was wrong.

God loved me when I failed,

and when I was far from him he wasn't far from me.

He was waiting,

anxious for me to accept his love.

   He knows I fail,

and that I'll fail again tomorrow,

and again all my life.

But he still loves me . . . no matter what.

I'm hardest on myself, really.

    I set standards:

I want to be a certain kind of person,

a person to please my friends,

to please God,

to please my parents,

to please the college admissions boards,

to please someone.

    And when I don't measure up, I hate myself.

For days.

I'm worse than my parents.

I'm worse than the church.

I'm worse than my friends.

They forget, and they forgive.

    But I have a hard time forgiving myself.

    I can still remember stupid things

I did in the fifth grade.

    God could, too.

He has every right to.

It's not that he doesn't care what I act like.

It's that his love is unconditional.

No matter how often I fail,

I cannot make God stop caring for me.

Nor can I pay him back for his love by acting right.

All I can do is say "Thank you."

And be grateful.

What about being good?

Isn't it important to measure up to my potential?

To be the kind of friend I should?

to be the kind of person I should?

Doesn't that matter to God?

Yes, it matters.

But it is not what his love depends on.

Nothing I could ever do would be enough

to make God love me.

You cannot *make* him love anyone.

He just does.

TIM STAFFORD

You see, at just the right time, when we were still powerless, Christ died for the ungodly. Very rarely will anyone die for a righteous man, though for a good man someone might possibly dare to die. But God demonstrates his own love for us in this: While we were still sinners, Christ died for us.
ROMANS 5:6-8

For I am convinced that neither death nor life, neither angels nor demons, neither the present nor the future, nor any powers, neither height nor depth, nor anything else in all creation, will be able to separate us from the love of God that is in Christ Jesus our Lord.
ROMANS 8:38, 39

You work terribly hard to win the approval of peers, teachers, coaches, parents. And that's not a bad thing: You can do worse than trying to be the best person possible. The problem is, anyone who gets to know you well will eventually see the "other" you. The you you're not so proud of. That's when you'll know what kind of friend you have on your hands.

A friend who expects you to be perfect isn't much of a friend, because no matter how hard you try, you can't live up to that expectation. At least not all the time.

It may be hard to believe, but God doesn't love you because he thinks you're perfect. In fact, only God knows just how imperfect you are. He loves you because he wants to. He loves you because his Son died for you. Love like that is freeing; it allows you to try and fail. It allows you to make mistakes and learn from them. It allows you to ask for forgiveness and carry on. God doesn't want you to berate yourself for being 100 percent human; he created you that way. He wants you to accept the great delight and love he has for you, and to get on with becoming more like him in every aspect of your personality.

Dear God, thank you for loving me just as I am. Help me to love myself, to enjoy being me, and to accept others with the same kind of love. Amen.

NO MATTER WHAT

III.

Remember when Linda

made me the cookies? Or the time

when all my friends woke me up at 6:00 A.M.

and went out for a breakfast party?

Did you know how happy I was, how grateful I felt?

For days I wanted to do things for them.

Not because I owed it.

Just because they had loved me,

and I loved them back.

   "Just because you love him."

This is the only motive Jesus wants to see us

"acting good" in.

And it is also the only motive

that will help me be

what he wants, day after day.

   All other motives

for being good

get tired

and worn out.

Sometimes you just

rebel and do

something stupid.

But when you really

love someone,

it goes on forever.

No matter what.

TIM STAFFORD

This is love: not that we loved God, but that he loved us and sent his Son as an atoning sacrifice for our sins. And so we know and rely on the love God has for us. God is love. Whoever lives in love lives in God, and God in him. There is no fear in love. But perfect love drives out fear, because fear has to do with punishment. The man who fears is not made perfect in love. We love because he first loved us.

1 JOHN 4:10, 16, 18, 19

I have loved you with an everlasting love; I have drawn you with loving-kindness.

JEREMIAH 31:3

Our actions don't always issue from the purest motives. Sometimes we act nicely around adults or important peers because we fear them. After all, they can make life difficult for us. At other times we exhibit care and concern just to maintain our reputations. It's a show, and if we could be sure no one was watching . . . But God is watching, and he knows when we're playing at being good for all the wrong reasons. We can deceive other people and perhaps even ourselves. We can't deceive God.

The acts of love we display toward special friends are genuine. Then we love because we want to, and because the love we give out is returned to us. God's love is like that. He's heaped it upon us, even when we don't deserve it. To acknowledge God's love is to return it to him and to other people. In that sense, God's good acts toward us are never really lost. They're in a cycle that can only stop with us.

Dear God, help me to be more aware of my motives for loving others. Teach me how to share the pure love you have given to me. Amen.

ROOTED

Life is full of forces,
Forces that make me like a blade of grass—

    dried

    detached

    carried along by a breeze.

    Its direction depends on the wind.

    It rests for a while

    until the next gust comes along

    and carries it somewhere else;

    no direction

    no weight of its own

    completely at the mercy of outside forces.

God, I need inside force.

    Give me whatever it takes to make a tree stand

    the sap that makes it live

    the roots that keep it anchored

    no matter how hard the wind is blowing.

Show me the rivers

    where I can put my roots down deep.

Give me the courage of a tree

    Make me more than a blade of dried grass.

RUTH SENTER

Blessed is the man who does not walk in the counsel of the wicked or stand in the way of sinners or sit in the seat of mockers. But his delight is in the law of the Lord, and on his law he meditates day and night. He is like a tree planted by streams of water, which yields its fruit in season and whose leaf does not wither. Whatever he does prospers. Not so the wicked! They are like chaff that the wind blows away. Therefore the wicked will not stand in the judgment, nor sinners in the assembly of the righteous. For the Lord watches over the way of the righteous, but the way of the wicked will perish.

PSALM 1

Ever see a stretch of maritime forest? Its trees are misshapen, bent by years of prevailing ocean winds. Twisted limbs, scraggly foliage—it seems that a few good gusts would uproot the whitewashed ghosts. But these trees are survivors; their roots reach into the sandy soil so deeply that they are not threatened by winds that strip their branches and bend their trunks. Even gale winds and hurricanes do little damage to a stretch of maritime forest.

We need to be strong like trees, especially when life whips at us with hurricane force. Without an adequate understanding of God and ourselves, we are at the mercy of forces much greater than we can humanly bear. But if we are rooted, our experiences—great and small—will mark us as people able to endure. Only in God can we sink our roots deep enough to withstand life's prevailing winds.

Dear God, sink me deep in you. Give me courage to accept and live out my life in a way pleasing to you. Amen.

ONE MORE TIME

God,
you make me feel like I did
when my ninth-grade history teacher
postponed our semester exam at the last minute,
giving us an extra twenty-four hours
to study

When I sliced a pop foul to the catcher
with the bases loaded
in the conference championship game
and watched as he lost the ball in the sun

When I awoke from a bad dream
in which I'd committed murder
and realized
that I hadn't planted a bomb
after all

The time I fell asleep
at the wheel
and awoke just in time
to come to a screeching halt
at a busy intersection

Thanks

for being a God

who gives second chances.

TERRY POWELL

Praise the Lord, O my soul; all my inmost being, praise his holy name. Praise the Lord, O my soul, and forget not all his benefits. He forgives all my sins and heals all my diseases; he redeems my life from the pit and crowns me with love and compassion.

PSALM 103:1-4

He who has been forgiven little loves little.

LUKE 7:47

God always gives us another chance. His willingness to allow us to try and fail—again and again—is evidence of his great love for us. God doesn't make us do anything his way; he only asks us to. And when we instead do it our way, and fail, and plead our humanness, God forgives us without saying, "I told you so."

God gives us so many second and third and fourth chances that we should readily be gracious toward those who fail us. But we more often respond with anger and hurt. We build walls to protect ourselves; we cut people off. "Once is enough. I won't let you fail me again," we say, forgetting how much we have been forgiven. Forgetting how much we have hurt God. Forgetting how much we need another chance. Forgetting our common humanness.

Dear God, thank you for forgiving me countless times over, for not turning away when I fail you. Remind me of your constant love-in-action when others fail me. Amen.

THE WIND

The Wind

of the Spirit is blowing.

Lift me, Lord, and let me soar with the speed of time,

    content to see the dust of yesterday bury the past.

Chase the wind with me,

Dream with me,

Yesterday is gone and can't be held by wishes.

Now is the time for vision and for prayer.

This is a day for new adventures

        I do rejoice,

                and I am glad.

                       MARILEE ZDENEK

Teach us to number our days aright, that we may gain a heart of wisdom.

               PSALM 90:12

This is the day the Lord has made; let us rejoice and be glad in it.

               PSALM 118:24

How many nights have you stayed awake worrying about something you did that seemed, in retrospect, foolish? Sometimes we lose sleep because we feel guilty but don't want to face what we've done. When you know you've mistreated someone, you can clear your mind by asking first for God's forgiveness and then for the injured person's. The longer you deny your guilt, the more difficult it will be to step toward reconciliation. And your pride can become so great that you never move at all.

What about times when you can't put your finger on anything wrong, yet the memory of acting foolishly or inappropriately makes you uncomfortable? Take time to think through the situation. Why did you act as you did? Were you feeling a lack of confidence? Were you embarrassed, nervous, or too self-conscious? How can you do better next time?

No amount of effort will bring back yesterday. Confess and learn from your past, and get on with the future.

Dear God, thank you for giving me this new day. May I grow as you intend through its experiences. Amen.

RIDER

Yesterday

      (flashing second)

my horse broke from me.

Pounding pounding

flew the hoofs.

Hands tearing,

I clung

as the massive weight

      plunged

low

to earth's grave

then up, up

reached for the sky.

Today,

      rubbing bruised

arm's flesh, I

became the run-

away. Sin

must yet be broken.

ANDREA MIDGETT

Do not offer the parts of your body to sin, as instruments of wickedness, but rather offer yourselves to God, as those who have been brought from death to life; and offer the parts of your body to him as instruments of righteousness. For sin shall not be your master.

ROMANS 6:13, 14

No one who is born of God will continue to sin, because God's seed remains in him; he cannot go on sinning, because he has been born of God.

1 JOHN 3:9

Gaining control of a runaway horse can be a frightening experience, even for a seasoned rider. As the animal gathers momentum, rearing and trying to rid itself of the person on its back, the rider must work harder and harder to rein its head in. Falling or being thrown overhead and underfoot at such speed can be deadly.

Sin is like a runaway horse; it wants its own way in our lives. Once we've relinquished control, even in little areas, it will begin to take the lead. The Christian's only hope in conquering sin is to submit to Christ as Lord. Asking him to be in charge of every area of our lives isn't easy—we like to think we can battle the power and influence of sin on our own. But left to ourselves, we eventually will be overcome by something much stronger than us. And left to itself, sin always leads to death.

Dear God, please be master of my life. Place my desires and whole being under your control. Amen.

TIME LAPSE

The clock ran backwards.

Clearly.

Unmistakably.

From the beginning

it had measured life spans with unnerving precision.

Then it stopped.

Abruptly.

The hands locked motionless for three long days

as if enshrouded.

But when it shuddered to life again,

it ran backwards.

Clearly.

Unmistakably.

And death itself convulsed.

JIM LONG

This man was handed over to you by God's set purpose and foreknowledge; and you, with the help of wicked men, put him to death by nailing him to the cross. But God raised him from the dead, freeing him from the agony of death, because it was impossible for death to keep its hold on him. David said about him: "I saw the Lord always before me. Because he is at my right hand, I will not be shaken. Therefore my heart is glad and my tongue rejoices; my body also will live in hope, because you will not abandon me to the grave, nor will you let your Holy One see decay. You have made known to me the paths of life; you will fill me with joy in your presence."

ACTS 2:23-28

Do you forget that your God is the God of the Bible, the master and shaper of history? The God who led King David, who forgave and enthroned and befriended him, leads you. The God who entered the human sphere in the person of his Son lives within you. The God who moved the clock back and brought life from the grave will keep your soul from death.

God did not abandon his people in the Old Testament when they responded to him with disobedience and neglect. His plans for redeeming mankind were not defeated by the death of his Son. Why do you fear that he will abandon the plans he has for you? God has clearly worked in your behalf until now. He will continue to direct you according to his will. What he has purposed, he will never abandon, even if it means moving time backwards.

Dear God, thank you for being a God of power and might, of purpose and faithfulness. Thank you for being the God of history, and the God of me. Amen.

MY FRIEND

She has acne. And moods.

She says she is Going through a Phase. She is trying to Get

Her Head Together.

She doesn't like parents or teachers or the police.

If I had a treasure, I'd give her a goodly share so she could

take a trip around the world and wear out her phase.

But I don't have a treasure so:

I'll give her a smile.

I'll listen to her gripes about the injustices of life.

And sometimes I'll laugh with her, and sometimes I'll cry with

her,

but I'll be her friend.

I'll show her honesty. And loyalty.

And I won't lose patience with her—I hope.

ROBERTA STROTKAMP

He has alienated my brothers from me; my acquaintances are completely estranged from me. My kinsmen have gone away; my friends have forgotten me. My guests and my maidservants count me a stranger; they look upon me as an alien. I summon my servant, but he does not answer, though I beg him with my own mouth. My breath is offensive to my wife; I am loathsome to my own brothers. Even the little boys scorn me; when I appear, they ridicule me. All my intimate friends detest me; those I love have turned against me. I am nothing but skin

and bones; I have escaped with only the skin of my teeth.
Have pity on me, my friends, have pity, for the hand of God
has struck me. Why do you pursue me as God does? Will you
never get enough of my flesh?

JOB 19:13-22

This is how we know what love is: Jesus Christ laid down his
life for us. And we ought to lay down our lives for our brothers.

1 JOHN 3:16

Οne of Job's most difficult trials was the fickleness of his friends. Job thought they would stand beside him during his time of need, but they didn't. And what they did was worse than quietly forsaking the afflicted man—Job's friends rubbed salt in his wounds by blaming him for his predicament.

Christ teaches that real love is being willing to die for your friends. He doesn't say anything about your friends' returning the favor. Think of his friendships with men and women: He was ridiculed, misunderstood, accused of blasphemy. Some of his friends stood by him faithfully—until doing so placed their lives in jeopardy. Then they, too, deserted him. He, on the other hand, lived out his friendships to the point of death. When you're struggling to be a good friend, think of Christ, the perfect model. To give of yourself is to love with his love.

Dear God, thank you for the
friendship Christ offers to all
people. Help me be the kind of
friend that he is. Amen.

PRIORITY MAIL

You came to me

In words

Written on yellow sheets of

Notebook paper

Inked in blue

Folded and stuffed

In a plain, white envelope

Lots of letters

Come and go

In my post office box

But only one

Matters:

The one that brings

You

To me

I know the writing

Tear open the seal

Time stops

Even people wait

There is just

You

And me

And the letter

I find a place without people

A solitary spot under a birch tree

To read about

You

And me

And us

I belong to those words

To the one who penned

The neat block letters

I look for you behind the lines

Where are you as you write?

What are your feelings?

What are your thoughts?

What were you doing

Before you wrote?

What will you do

When you are done?

I look for meaning

I read between the lines

In search of

Your love

In search of

The you that I love

I read again

The same words

But new information

Four times

Over the yellow pages

With blue block letters

And I've missed half of lunch

But nothing matters

Except

You are here with me

In words

Delivered in a twenty-two–cent envelope

That seems like gold

But imagine:

An unopened letter

From the one

You love

Imagine:

Unread correspondence

From the God

You love

RUTH SENTER

I meditate on your precepts and consider your ways. I delight in your decrees; I will not neglect your word.

For everything that was written in the past was written to teach us, so that through endurance and the encouragement of the Scriptures we might have hope.

ROMANS 15:4

All Scripture is God-breathed and is useful for teaching, rebuking, correcting and training in righteousness, so that the man of God may be thoroughly equipped for every good work.

2 TIMOTHY 3:16

Few things are worse than waiting for the postman to deliver the day's mail. You walk to the front door, look in the box, and then look down the street. No one in sight. Five, ten minutes later, you repeat the scene. Open the door. Look out. If it's past the usual delivery time, you grow irritated. And if, when the mail finally comes, there is nothing from that friend you so much want (and need) to hear from, you become deadly depressed.

What's so special about a letter? Anyone can put pen to paper, scratch out a sentence or two, fold the message and stuff it in an envelope, stamp it. Anyone can, but only friends do. Bill collectors send notices. Advertisers send pamphlets. Only friends have the dedication consistent letter writing requires. Letters between friends are a unique type of communication. Friends come to life in the words they choose. The Bible is God's letter to us, a letter to read and ponder and reread. To read God's letter strengthens our understanding of and friendship with him. It should be priority mail.

Dear God, thank you for communicating with me through written words. May I be a faithful reader of your correspondence. Amen.

184

YOU

You are the healing

the loving

the touching

You are the laughing

the dancing

Jesus Verb of God

You are the moving

move in me

MARILEE ZDENEK

For in him we live and move and have our being.
ACTS 17:28

I am come that they may have life, and have it to the full.
JOHN 10:10

*You, O Lord, keep my lamp burning; my God turns my
darkness into light.*
PSALM 18:28

Ever feel that you're stuck in neutral? That you're lifeless, without energy for joy and laughter and love? More than ever, that's when you need to remember that as a Christian you are united to the giver of life. God created you as a whole person; he wants you to be alive psychologically, physically, intellectually, and spiritually. Don't discredit God by acting as though he's concerned only with your spiritual well-being.

You can ask God to energize you and fill you with himself in any situation. You can call on him no matter how low you feel. That's what the "full life" that Jesus promises his followers is all about—a life full of his presence and power. Jesus, who defeated the power of evil and death, understands your needs. Your relationship to him automatically ties you into God's strength and power and activity. You have an eternal life source. Tap into it.

Dear God, thank you for caring about the complete me. Give me a sense of your presence and activity and fullness of life in every aspect of my being. Amen.

THE SUN GOES DOWN ON SUMMER

It's a warm, silent sea

of thought dyed in the rich blues

of night and memory

    come to the water one last time

    as the sun goes down on summer.

It's going; I can feel it slip away,

and it leaves a cold, empty spot,

    a hole in my warm memories of endless golden days

    and dreams as ripe as watermelons.

I'd give the world to make the summer stay.

The water is calm around me.

It's a warm, silent sea of thought

dyed in the rich blues of night

and memory.

Why can't things just stay the way they are?

Instead, the days rush headlong into change

and I feel like nothing's ever going to be the same.

Soon school will start again.

And all the things I thought I'd left behind will come back,

    and it won't be gentle water I'll be swimming in—

    it'll be noise and people and schedules and

        teachers telling everyone what to do.

Another year of homework,

        tests

        and grades.

        Of daily popularity contests

        and pressure-cooker competition

        and heaps of frustration.

The first day is the worst. Not knowing

        who your friends are,

        or what's changed since last year.

        Trying to

pick up where you left off.

I'll look real hard for a last-year's friend or a face I know

    to get me from one scrambled class to another,

      through halls crawling with people.

I wonder if I'll fit in.

Football practice started last week.

    It started without me.

I had to make a choice and football lost.

Two years on the team and it struck me: who am I doing this for?

    It's just another thing people expect you to do,

    so you do it.

School is full of those kinds of things—

    things that sap your freedom,

    and keep you from being yourself.

That's what I want most.

　　To be myself.

　　But that's hard.

Here's what I dread most:

　　when summer goes, I go with it.

I go back to school and I change as soon as I walk through those

doors.

I have to be someone everyone will like—

that's a law of survival.

What would happen if I just stayed the real me?

Would they turn me off?

Label me "weird"?

Would I ever get another date?

It seems like so much to risk.

　　But growing is a risk.

　　Change is a risk.

And who knows,

　　I might discover something of myself in the coming year.

　　I might get closer to the person I am.

When the doors open on Monday morning,

　　I'll have a fresh start,

　　a fresh opportunity to find myself.

I want to be ready.

STEVE LAWHEAD

Then we will no longer be infants, tossed back and forth by the waves, and blown here and there by every wind of teaching and by the cunning and craftiness of men in their deceitful scheming. Instead, speaking the truth in love, we will in all things grow up into him who is the Head, that is, Christ.

EPHESIANS 4;14, 15

When anxiety was great within me, your consolation brought joy to my soul.

PSALM 94:19

Growth can be scary and uncomfortable, for it depends on change. Think of how awkward and clumsy your body has been at times of growth. Or think of how disappointed and afraid you were to abandon favorite childhood beliefs (tooth fairies, parents who never make mistakes). To grow as an individual you must look honestly at the world and at yourself.

In God's scheme each person has a place in the world, each has something to contribute. And that includes you. Your interests and tastes and combination of friends do not exactly match those of any other person. Your background and abilities (and disabilities) have equipped you to respond to different situations as no one else can. God desires that you be the person he created you to be; if he had wanted you to be someone else, he would have created you as someone else. The option is to be indistinguishable—just like everyone else—in a safe, unchanging world.

Dear God, help me put away beliefs and fears that keep me from personal growth. May I see myself and others with honest eyes. Amen.

ABOUT FACE

Turn me around, Lord—

I have no idea where I'm going,

and the only things I'm sure about

are my doubts.

My prayers are mumbled fragments,

by-products of indecision.

I want to face myself,

but the strength drains away

as I run from my problems.

I need you, Lord—

don't look the other way.

You're my fulfillment,

not my crutch.

Turn me around, Lord,

so I can see where I'm going.

LOIS BREINER

Therefore, get rid of all moral filth and the evil that is so prevalent, and humbly accept the word planted in you, which can save you. Do not merely listen to the word, and so deceive yourselves. Do what it says. Anyone who listens to the word but does not do what it says is like a man who looks at his face in a mirror and, after looking at himself, goes away and immediately forgets what he looks like. But the man who

***looks intently into the perfect law that gives freedom, and
continues to do this, not forgetting what he has heard, but
doing it—he will be blessed in what he does.***

You can do one of two things
after seeing yourself for who you really are. You can work on
changing the unsatisfactory parts of your personality—the
jealousy, the bitterness, the desire to be first in everything, the bad
habits. Or you can do nothing—and grow worse. Regardless of the
action you decide upon, you'll be moving. You're not the same
person you were yesterday, and in some small or significant way,
you'll be a different person tomorrow.

While losing ground doesn't require much effort, personal
growth demands strength and insight. It's like going uphill on
cross-country skis; simply not paying attention can catapult you to
the bottom. God wants you to move in the right direction, and he's
willing to guide you every step of the way. But he won't take the
lead until you ask him to.

***Dear God, take the lead in
transforming every aspect of my
being, that I may become more
like your Son who lives within
me. Give me your strength,
determination, and love of
holiness. Amen.***

A CAPSULE OF BELIEF

Christians believe in God the Maker . . .

    an invisible Father behind everything that exists . . .

who made the first art, carving abstractions in cliffs,

    or forming the soft kaleidoscope of changing expressions in

    a baby's face . . .

who made the stars that dust the sky, behemoths gorging

    themselves on gases, collapsing into the dark hell-heat of

    a black hole, or exploding in waves of violence . . .

who had the idea of making men and women different,

    and then brought the differences together in an ecstatic

    expression we call sex . . .

who made man to long for him. . . .

Christians believe in Jesus . . .

    a human being with the audacity to claim that he and God

    were the same, and doing the same work . . .

whose leadership flared for three brilliant years under

    the Roman Empire, and then burned out (seemingly) in a Roman

    execution . . .

who reappeared, alive, three days after dying . . .

who lives now holding atoms together,

    giving permission for each breath . . .

who expects us to listen to him, and love him, as leader . . .

whose leadership, now invisible, will someday be impossible to
deny. . . .

Christians believe in God's Spirit . . .
who breathes the words "you are special" to anyone who
    invites God to reorder his life . . .
who offers the strength to love God and any person we
    meet . . . to sacrifice our own interests in his or her
favor, something
    we could never do by ourselves . . .
who comforts and encourages, who points the right way to
    go when we are confused, who pulls our thoughts together . . .
who is God's special, personal self on earth. . . .

Christians believe in people . . .
who out of all the systems in the universe, all swinging
    planets, powerful oaks, padding lions, chattering apes,
        were given the gift of choice: to love or ignore God . . .
who know, deepest of all creatures, what the word
    "love" means . . .
who also know the despair that comes without love . . .
who are meant to be God-chosen creatures, knowing and living
    with the One who gives love its definition (for God is love) . . .
whom God judges worth giving up everything for, even
    his own Son. For the planet-maker Jesus died trying

to bring us to our senses . . .

whom God loves, no matter what.

TIM STAFFORD

There is one body and one Spirit—just as you were called to one hope when you were called—one Lord, one faith, one baptism; one God and Father of all, who is over all and through all and in all.

EPHESIANS 4:4-6

That which was from the beginning, which we have heard, which we have seen with our eyes, which we have looked at and our hands have touched—this we proclaim concerning the Word of life. The life appeared; we have seen it and testify to it, and we proclaim to you the eternal life, which was with the Father and has appeared to us. We proclaim to you what we have seen and heard, so that you also may have fellowship with us. And our fellowship is with the Father and with his Son, Jesus Christ.

1 JOHN 1:1-3

Christians agree on many things. And Christians disagree on many things. But though the customs and practices of American Baptists and Polish Catholics and Japanese Presbyterians differ, the foundation of each group's faith is the same. It is the shared beliefs of all Christians that bind us to each other, worldwide. When we know what we believe, and why, we recognize others whose beliefs are essentially the same. For example, baptism by immersion or sprinkling is debatable, yet all believers agree on the significance of baptism. Whether one goes to the altar for communion, or passes the bread and wine (or grape juice, another difference) up and down the pews may rest largely on tradition. Remembering Christ's death is the command. As

Christians, we confess Jesus as Lord and Savior. We believe in one God; we are confirmed in our faith by one Spirit.

Perhaps it's pride, but it's easy to think of our own church or denomination or youth group as the best. We must constantly guard against judging others who worship differently from us, looking instead for the binding elements of our faith. It's not that the other points of doctrine and biblical interpretation aren't important. They are, and they have practical implications. But we should look first at the cornerstone of our faith, Jesus Christ. He'll put all else in proper perspective.

Dear God, forgive me for being critical of other believers who don't worship exactly as I do. And help me to discover joyfully the common elements of my faith and my Christian brother's or sister's. Amen.